AN M-Y BOOK

A CIP catalogue record for this title is
available from the British Library

ISBN 13 digit – 9781906986728

Published by
M-Y Books LTD
187 Ware Road
Hertford
Herts SG13 7EQ

Design and layout by

caroline@sparkleforyou.co.uk

A Journey Of Awakening

Taking The Other Road

By Ron Farquhar

Contents

Prelude

Cuckoos

The boy walked slowly by the hedge, holding a loaded catapult, looking for birds in range to kill. It was mid-May and very hot, with few trees to give him shade.

On the other side of the hedge were some large buildings where the Territorial Army did their drill. The grounds were used as a firing range and also for bayonet practice, with dummy men hanging from wooden frames. Through gaps in the hedge he would often watch them, running at the dummies, shouting loudly before sticking bayonets in the swinging, lifeless effigies. His father was in the Royal Artillery Regiment and glad he didn't have to do this kind of thing.

The gang decided to see who was the best shot. Though he'd killed many birds that year, he never cheated, counting only those he'd seen fall and picked up. Once he had killed a bird in full flight - his best shot ever. He never found that one, but saw the feathers fall and heard the unmistakable sound as the stone struck home. Once, he and a friend found a tawny owl roosting in a small tree. Because he'd read it was unlucky to kill owls, he only pretended to aim … the owl flew off and was then mobbed by other birds.

Tired of looking along the hedge, he jogged towards the main road. The stones in his pocket swung as he ran, making it difficult to balance and causing some to fall out. He found that steadying them with his hand made running easier. When he reached the road he looked either way and then crossed to the cinder path - his favourite area for birds and a source of good stones. The silver birches, coupled with a chestnut fence about four feet high, formed a natural avenue; the path led to the factory where his father had worked before the war came. On his left were sand pits that had been in use since the time of Henry VIII to provide ballast to help ships navigate the Thames. On reaching the area where the good stones lay, he deftly picked the roundest and heaviest, then fired a few at the fence just to hear the force of the impact as they thwacked hard into the thin upright staves. He did the same to the tarmac path, hearing the whine as the stone ricocheted into the air, as bullets do when cowboys fire their guns in films.

Squeezing his way through a gap in the fence, and placing the left side of his body first to allow the stones room, he went into the overgrown area where there was sand and half-dug caves. He was careful of the low brambles, for his legs were only partially covered with grey socks. Wending his way though the tangled briars he stood on them to avoid scratches. He walked slowly, with the catapult ready loaded, carefully placing his feet on the uneven ground as he looked for birds.

Suddenly a rabbit darted for cover amidst the low brambles. He followed, running fast through the sharp-toothed briars. He fired the stone as he kept up the chase, stumbling as he went, anxious to get the rabbit - but it had disappeared. Looking down at his legs he saw they were scratched in all directions, with blood running from the deepest wounds. He pulled up his socks, easing the pain a little. Some of the stones were shaken from his pocket as he tripped, but he felt he had enough to last the mission. Reloading the weapon, he used a wider path away from the briars, feeling less threatened by them.

He would have loved to hit the rabbit. Perhaps the stone might have stunned it? Then he could have pulled its neck, just like the farmer did in the place where he was evacuated. The man held its back legs and head, until its neck cracked and went limp. His mother could have cooked it or sold it to someone.

Such were his thoughts as he settled down to watch the woods from his hiding place. Formed by the extraction of the sand a long time ago, it was his secret lair which no one else knew about. Now it was overgrown with low bushes and small trees.

He found the right spot with soft grass under a silver birch. Lowering his socks to remove the briars from his legs, he was fearful of pushing them deeper into his flesh. It was difficult removing some of them - his nails weren't long enough to get a proper grip. Tired from the effort of concentration, he lay back on the grass and forced himself to look through the branches at the sun, which made him squint.

Hearing a cuckoo he reloaded his catapult, straining hard to see it. How he'd love to kill a cuckoo: none of his friends had ever done that. Suddenly it was in the tree above him. He was afraid to move in case it flew away. Then again, *'cuckoo, cuckoo, cuckoo'*: but he couldn't see it and so lost the chance to kill it – the chance to prevent other birds from dying, when laying eggs in their nests. The young cuckoo would soon grow quickly and push out the other birds as it grew too big for the nest. Why couldn't he see it when it was so close? Elated at having the privilege of one so near, he fired some more stones towards the sand-pit, releasing the anger he felt at missing his chance to kill the cuckoo. Then, moving from his hide-out, he folded back the bushes to hide the gap he had made, trying not to leave any sign that he'd been there.

Arriving home and finding his mother out, he could still smell the powder and strong scent she'd used. He wrapped the catapult in his handkerchief and hid it under the bath, knowing it would be safe. His dinner was on the stove, kept warm by hot water in a pot under the plate. He was hungry and wasted no time in lifting the plate with a cloth, as he had seen his mother do many times. Once he tried this but was too slow, catching the full force of the escaping steam on his wrists, which made him scream with the pain. Soon learnt a lesson!

It was dark now, so he made sure the blackout curtains were closed, and then put his feet up on the side of the armchair before listening to music on the radio. Turning the light and radio off, he opened a curtain but saw nothing but blackness until, looking at the sky, he saw a sliver of moon behind a cloud with faint stars. It was hard to discern through the small window. He was soon asleep, thinking of the rabbit and the cuckoo.

Later, woken by the sound of singing, he heard his mother's high pitched voice, then silence. Knowing what was to come next - the key in the lock then the hurried steps as she came up the stairs into his room; her bending over him and speaking in a soft voice, calling his name - he smelt the hated drink and scent. His eyes were closed, feigning sleep, waiting for her to go away. She went quickly to the friends she had left waiting with the men. There was subdued giggling as they entered the house; soon there was the tinkling of glasses as drink was passed around. His thoughts went to the bottles and the money he would get when returning them for the deposits. Sometimes he waited until it was silent, then made his way down the stairs and took money from the men's jackets as they hung from the doors in the hallway. Taking a little from each, aware that if he took more he could be discovered, he hid it under the bath ready to take to school the next day. Soon he drifted off to sleep; too tired to do as he'd planned, knowing there would be other times.

Next morning he woke to the voice of the Irish tenor, John McCormack. Liking his voice, he ran quickly down the stairs to get closer to the radio, hearing one of his favourites, *Jeanie with the light brown hair*. Listening … as his mother cleared the mess of the night's drinking. He saw seven or eight bottles tucked behind the door; feeling some pleasure; deciding what to do with the money. The smell of food being cooked and the home being cleaned gave him a secure feeling, taking away the smell of sweat and sex. He couldn't understand how she could do it, with his father away.

That morning he somehow felt closer to her, feeling comfortable and cared for. When the breakfast was ready she gave it to him, as he sprawled on the chair. She began to polish the brass fender placed on the top of the table. Underneath were old newspapers - these helped prevent fluid falling on the chenille tablecloth. Behind the fender stood four chairs stacked seat-to-seat, which had been polished till they sparkled from her hard rubbing. The boy took the plate to the kitchen, leaving it on the draining board. Opening the pantry door as a matter of habit, he looked for cakes or anything that took his fancy. When he returned to the front room, the windows had been opened. The fresh air coupled with the smell of polish cleared the house of the activities of the previous night, making it clean to live in.

* * * *

Most Sundays he visited his grandmother at Castle Terrace, a small row of two-up, two-down condemned properties in Slades Green, to have dinner with his aunts. His grandmother made him welcome, as did other travelling girls, finding him different, coming from a better-off part of the town. His grandmother sold flowers that she bought from local nurseries. Sometimes she told him where to collect golden rod, a wild plant that she mixed with others she'd bought.

* * * *

The catapult had become a part of him: he was never without it. Birds were his most desired targets. The catapult was his weapon, giving him the power to strike at anything. This somehow gave him relief from his inner confusion and pain. Deeper within lay an affinity with music, singing and the written word, but he rarely gave vent to these feelings.

He often returned to where he'd seen the cuckoo, the place of escape from the problems of war. But he never saw another one. Now older, with a criminal record, he had eventually left the district and was married, with children of his own.

Once, when trying to unravel his disturbed psyche by going to various groups, he was asked by the seminar leader to think of a safe place he could unshackle any burdens he'd been carrying during the course of his life. He felt again the grass between his fingers, eyes closed, letting the sun warm his face, listening to the birds in this secret place, far from the mundane business of life. He allowed his body to relax as he said "Just let birdsong trill in enchantment for you." 'Cuckoo, Cuckoo, Cuckoo'.

Now, smiling and content to re- live the memory of childhood, seeing the sun through the silver birch, feeling it warm every pore of his body, oblivious to the pain of the once barbed thorns, he heard once again the calls of the cuckoo.

Early Years in Erith

*I go to different garbage and scuffle for scraps of
notice*
*Pretend to ignore the stigma that stains my life and
leisure.*
For fretful even in leisure, I fidget for different values.
*Restless as a gull and haunted, by a hankering after
Atlantis*
*I do not know that Atlantis unseen and
uncomprehending.*
Dimly divined but keenly felt with a phantom hunger.
*If I could only crush the hunger, if only I could lay the
phantom*
*Then I should no doubt be happy like a fool a dog or a
Buddha*
Mc Niece.

I was born in the Hainault Maternity Hospital, Erith,
Kent, on the 8th January 1932; conceived on a bed of
cushions hurriedly made up for Sophie the Gypsy
flower seller my father had plied with drink, after
inviting her to his house for his sister Flo's 21st
Birthday Party, April 6th 1931.

Sophie was twenty, the eldest of nine, and had helped
bring up six sisters and two brothers: the norm for
large families at the time. In consequence she never
went to school: acting as a surrogate mother she

sacrificed her own education for the benefit of the younger siblings.

My father added another name to the tally of local girls he'd seduced. But that night was not forgotten. Those who take advantage of virgins, particularly those from travelling families, have to pay for their actions. My mother's father was not a man to be made a fool of so, much to the anger of my father's family, the marriage took place.

My father's six sisters and brother, Claude, thought the flower seller far too beneath them, as she lived on the *Marsh* - a home for the lowest of the low where thieves and Diddicoys lived with a mix of Romany people and others without identity. This was an area of rough ground between Belvedere and Abbey Wood Railway Stations, owned by a travelling family. For years the council had tried to remove them but, as it was private property, the council's hands were tied: this is still the law today. It was an eyesore, consisting of caravans, defunct buses, and furniture vans: in fact anything water- tight that could be used to live in. The floods of 1953 removed them, much to the delight of Erith council and many others in a district that had suffered long enough from their presence.

Most of the people who lived there were resourceful, knowing how to scrape a living by selling whatever came to hand - logs, rag and bone merchants, old iron dealers - doing anything to exist that demanded guile, intelligence and energy. There were others of course who had none of the aforementioned attributes, so they stole if the opportunity arose. It was also a very dangerous place to live, for you had to cross railway lines by what was known as the *line gate*. From time to time there were fatal accidents involving children.

At the age of three I was taken there by my mother. It felt like a strange country, with men dressed in drab clothes sitting in circles staring at us, making me afraid. We stayed for a while in my grandmother's caravan then went into a shop made of wood, with a dirt floor and a high counter. When we left I had a temper tantrum, screaming obscenities as my mother dragged me along the rough dirt road, causing my shoes to fall off. Why I was upset I cannot remember, but even at that age I could only express it by acting in anger.

My father's family didn't live virtuous lives: my paternal Grandfather supplemented his income by stealing from his employers Cannon & Gaugley, flour wholesalers. His job was to deliver the flour to local bakers; the lorry used was a steam-driven type which had to have a full tank of water before leaving the yard. They would put just enough water in the tank to travel a few miles from the depot, then fill the tank with water from horse troughs that were common in those days. The weight of the water not put in at the depot would account for extra sacks of flour they added, so all would come out right on the weighbridge. The extra sacks would be sold off cheaply to the many bakers only too willing to get it for a lower price. I was told of this scam in my twenties, but it didn't surprise me after knowing my father better over the years. I realised he was no doubt influenced by his own father's actions, for he got into a few scrapes himself, stealing from places of work. Of the three people involved with this scam, two bought their own businesses, but my Grandfather, being a Scot, liked his whisky too much. He died suddenly of heart trouble in his mid-fifties and my mother made a wreath of a white dove going through the gates of heaven. He taught me how to ride my first Mickey Mouse tricycle and how to tie my laces. I still remember the wreath clearly.

My mother's family worked on the land, picking whatever was in season. During the winter months they would buy flowers from Convent Garden to sell in various markets. They also bought plants from nurseries, selling from door to door or offering them in return for clothing which they sold to stallholders, or exchanged among themselves if they fitted. These would be described as *getting out*. If any of the sisters admired what they were wearing, the retort would be, *"Yes, I got this out"*, meaning from the clothes they had collected when knocking door to door in the better-off streets.

They were not slow to steal if the opportunity arose. One particular stallholder who sold stockings at Erith market wasn't too alert. When his attention was elsewhere, my mother's sisters would poke what they could down their bloomers, which had been tied tight around their legs, allowing small packages to be taken. He would be described as a *Dinlo Mush* for being so stupid, allowing them to steal so easily.

As I grew older my grandmother would often tell me to be honest - not like Uncle Bert who was always involved with the law. Her favourite expression was, *"Don't you go hooking and crooking, like your Burtrum's. Keep on the straight road Ronnie, not the crooked one like him".* Though she was the only person to give me any moral guidance, I never heeded her advice. In my teens I always thought I would be able to outwit the police, unlike Bert who was always getting caught.

When I was born I was the biggest baby in the ward - nicknamed after the current heavyweight boxer Jack Dempsey - and with a double crown the nurse told my mother was a sign of intelligence. My first conscious memory was of pleasure and no pleasure. In effect, I was biting my mother's nipple with my first tooth and of course she'd remove it from my mouth. My mother later confirmed this occurrence when tracing back my early childhood with her.

My next memory was of faces coming and going in a frame. This was caused when my father's sisters took me for rides in a pram with the hood up, making a frame as I peered at them looking in at me, smiling as they did so. At the age of eighteen months, a most frightening experience occurred. There was a lot of shouting and noise as my mother's family tried to force the doors and windows of the house. My father never picked me up, but guided me from room to room; I was conscious of his fear and the tense atmosphere frightened me. Then, left alone in a room, I saw my mother smash her fist through the window, screaming in pain as she gashed her arm, making a deep wound that later formed a scar in the shape of a small horseshoe. I was in shock, trembling and screaming with fear at hearing her scream and the sound of the breaking glass. I have no other memories of the day, but assume the trouble was caused by my father's deceit - going with other women - for my sister Barbara was born about this time.

Later, nearing my fourth birthday, I went with a friend Charlie to a wood yard by the riverbank in West Street. It had a tar pit the size of a dustbin lid in circumference. We put all manner of objects into this Stygian goo, watching as they slowly disappeared after an initial plop: both fascinated where it went. I had nightmares about this place, fearing my own demise in this black pit. It wasn't till later, however, that I realised it was for dipping the ends of posts and gate supports.

My first silent film was about a boy who wanted to play a violin, but his rough, bullying, lumberjack father was annoyed and prevented him from playing it. I had sympathy for the boy who in the end, after various trials and setbacks, won the day and was allowed to play the instrument.

Going through a fairground late at night, at Erith Recreation ground, then to a market close by, there were men selling carrier bags of fruit from the backs of lorries. I was carried on the shoulders of my father and saw the whole area, lit with naphtha lights spluttering as the solution burnt in them, making it a place of wonder to my three-year-old bewildered eyes.

Before my fourth birthday, walking near West Street Infants' School, I was held spellbound as the pupils sang *All Things Bright and Beautiful*. I was entranced by the beauty of the voices and deeply moved by the experience … touching my young soul.

Though I later joined this school, I have little recollection of it other than when one day, walking home with a girl, I stuck the blade of my penknife in an apple on display in the front of a shop. She blurted out, *"You've stolen an apple, I shall tell teacher of you!!"* I had immediate visions of being hauled to the front of the school, named a thief and having to leave the place I had grown to love. The next day, too afraid to go to school, I stayed by the railway station playing on some waste ground amongst the undergrowth where I could hide. My aunt Doll came by and asked what I was doing there. Not believing my lame excuse, she said, "*A little bird tells me my lad that you are playing the wag my boy.*" I had immediate thoughts of being betrayed by a robin. I stayed away for another day but cannot recall any repercussions from the incident.

We moved to Cross Street, closer to the town, allowing a far wider area for me to roam. The river held a lot of interest - watching boats and playing on a small patch of shingle where I found chalk, when dried, could be used to draw on pavements, just as the other kids did who gathered there.

One day a man was giving free rides on his boat. I had just managed to get in as my mother called me. The fellow then asked, *"Was it your mother calling?"* I replied *"No",* feeling very guilty as I said it but eager to have my first ride on a boat. As it pulled away from the jetty my mother was still calling, her voice getting fainter as we went further along the river. For all my misbehaviour I was never hit by either of my parents, though my father would get near to it on those occasions when I would pester him for something or other. He would then shout very loudly - telling me to be quiet - which was enough to shut me up. My mother had a white wooden curtain rod that was kept behind a mirror on the wall above the fireplace. Although often threatened with it, I was never hit.

Our house on Cross Street was rat infested, and my mother attributed my brother John's ginger hair to having seen a ginger-coloured rat on the dresser, trying to take an egg from a glass bowl when she was pregnant with him. Travelling families have a habit of over dramatising innocuous situations, at the same time embellishing tales of long-dead relations, or those who have made money and are on too high a standard of living. They also deprecate each other in a critical way, which can sound humorous. My mother's sister, Mary, who had big lips, was called *'skates mouth'*, another tall aunt was known as *'the heron'*. My mother called me *'longshanks'*.

One Christmas, an old lady in the street gave me a small tree. It was about five inches tall, with white tinsel on the top representing snow. When I took it home to show my mother what I had been given and by whom, she replied, *"Oh! That's old mad Meg"*. I was taken aback at her retort because I found the woman generous and kind, even though she had a wart on her face with a grey hair growing from it.

We moved from a number of houses, staying only a short time in each. One was in Maximfeldt Road, behind the British Legion Club, where my mother first met my father who, at the time, was helping run the weekly dance. It was in this road that I made a friend of a boy my own age, Peter Salter. Something happened between us which caused me to hit him, making his nose bleed. We never spoke again, after his mother complained to mine. This was the first time I recall losing my temper and causing injury to another person. Other incidents occurred throughout my life: whenever I felt there had been a form of injustice I responded by losing my temper.

We were soon on the move again, but this time away from the town, to a house my father had to be vetted for. It was part of a new council project, moving people away from slum areas into above average housing. We went to Northumberland Heath. Known locally as *Spike Island,* you had to climb a variety of hills to get there. The house would have been described, in estate agent's jargon, as having three bedrooms, with front and back gardens, benefiting from a wonderful aspect from the rear windows, overlooking fields across the Thames to the Essex marshes, with the front enjoying a view of a private school's playing fields.

It was pure joy in the house, with a field at the back and orchards a short walk away. I was in my element, overawed by the contrast with Erith where I had felt so confined.

Ramsden Road was a mixture of working and lower-middle classes, but in the main the former, with rows frequently erupting among neighbours. We kids would listen to the rows, anxiously anticipating a fight to ensue. The pawnbrokers were used by some, including my mother, for now she had my brother John and sister Barbara to care for. The reason we were short of money was my father's inability to handle it. I had to take his suit in for pawning on a Monday then get it out for the weekend, as did others in the road.

I soon made friends with other boys but wanted to be part of the older gang as they seemed to be doing more interesting things. Once, when I asked to join them, they said, *"How fast can you run?"* I replied, *"Fast"*. They then said, *"Well run down the alley for us to see"*. I ran as fast as I could in my cheap Wellington boots. They all ran in the opposite direction, laughing at me for my foolishness. I never forgot the instigator of the prank.

It must have been in the winter, or at least late autumn, when moving to the Heath. I was intrigued at seeing clumps of black twigs in trees and was told they were nests. The following spring I found a nest, tucked between a post and an elderberry tree, that was part of the hedge surrounding an orchard. The beauty of the five blue eggs moved me to such rapture and awe - in the same way I had been moved by the voices, prior to joining the school. The following day, eager to see the nest again, I returned to find the eggs gone. My companion said, in a nonchalant way, that it had been ragged. I felt heartbroken by the disappearance of the eggs and the word *'ragged'* somehow described how I felt. It was the colour and beauty of the blue that enchanted me so.

My mother's family eventually came to visit, glad she had been so lucky to get the house. My aunt Emma told a joke about a black man who answered his door to the call of the dustman at the same time as he was putting a belt round his trousers. The dustman asked,

"Where's your bin?" The black man replied, *"I've been for a shit, where's you bin?"* There was much laughter over this, but all went quiet as my father came in very drunk and asked my mother to come up the stairs where I was lying on the bed. He said *"What are they doing here? I am going to f..ck you"*. She said, *"Yes all right don't start anything"* meaning not to cause any trouble. It was the only occasion I had ever seen my father behave in such a way and it lessened my opinion of him because of his language and attitude towards my mother and her family.

Another situation came about when trying to join the older boys' gang. A hole had been dug in the Orsler's back garden. They asked me to crawl through it, but halfway through I got stuck. To release myself I wriggled around forcing my left arm forward and cut it badly on a broken bottle protruding from the side. I ran to my house shouting for my mother to open the door, at the same time holding onto the arm, which had been cut to the bone. The door was locked and I was losing quite a lot of blood. I began to panic, knowing my mother was in but the door was closed tight. Later the blood stopped: in a few days a scab formed. I never told my mother about it for at the time she seemed too busy to ask. A woman in the road saw it and cleaned it up, dressing it with a bandage. I could only reason later that my mother was near to the birth of my youngest brother Bob and was having to put up with the attentions of my Father.

My first day at North Heath Infants' School was an occasion that gave me a lesson in life. My mother asked me not to cry, as big boys don't cry, so being a big boy I wouldn't cry. I was given some farm animals to play with that I found boring. The teacher was kind and helpful until I saw a large red aeroplane in the corner and began to play with it. I was promptly told, *"No! That's not for you"*. I didn't take too kindly to being refused the beckoning red toy when I hadn't cried.

The following day I was again given the farm animals. In the distance, a boy was bellowing his lungs out for all he was worth, refusing to enter the classroom, holding onto the door handle, determined not to come into the room. Eventually, with some bribery and cajoling, he came in and was immediately given the red plane. I felt the injustice of this action for I never cried and was given the farm animals. He screamed his head off to get the best of the toys. His name was Ken Vallis and I never forgave him for getting that plane, feeling once again the injustice of it.

When I was five, my father took me into town and bought some thin canes that had been treated with a green wood preservative. They were in a bundle of about twenty. Later in the night the sound of the canes and the low voices of my parents awakened me. The atmosphere was tense and fraught with the anticipation of danger. I was sleeping in a small bed beside theirs and felt as though I was involved in the situation. I could see my father under the bedclothes, using a torch to see what he was doing. I heard the word *'dangerous'* spoken a number of times but could not understand what was happening. I reasoned later that it was an attempted abortion that had fortunately failed. Bob was born the following August and I demanded that he was mine as we all ran into the bedroom eager too see our new addition. I kissed him so many times that by the time he was eighteen months old I had made a sore on his cheek.

Still trying to ingratiate myself with the older boys and gain their approval, I found myself with two of them in the redcurrant field. We had eaten our fill and they asked me to go and knock for a younger girl to see if she would come out to play. I did as they asked, only too glad to please them. The girl came out and we joined the other two, who immediately suggested that they play mothers and fathers. I sat watching as they each took turns to act the role of husband to the new-found wife, removing her knickers and enacting the movements of copulation with the innocent five-year-old girl, while counting in turn to a hundred. They didn't appear to have penetrated her, but enjoyed the act for what it was worth.

Some days elapsed and the astute pair asked me once again to get the same girl to see if she wanted to play. Her reply when opening the door was, *"I do not do that kind of thing anymore, because I have joined the Brownies"*. I recall another occasion when some older fellows erected a large tent at a place called *'The Wall'* by the Thames. Girls and fellows all shared this tent on a very hot summer's day, lying in pairs. Today, of course, the whole lot of them would have been hauled before the courts and charged with attempted sex with a minor, when in fact everything was an amicable lesson in growing up, causing no apparent harm at all to these pre-pubescent youths.

The War and Evacuation

You snare my path with trap and gin
Then blame me for my sin.
Omar Khayyam.

I was seven when war was declared. When the first practice siren sounded, women gathered by our back garden gate, talking about the forthcoming war. Soon there were air raid shelters being dug in each of the gardens along the road. There was also an attitude of *'Oh well, we had better get on with it'*.

It wasn't long before children were sent to various parts of Kent, taken from the areas of danger such as the Woolwich Arsenal munitions factory only a few miles distant.

My sister Barbara and I were packed off with our name-tagged gasmasks, condensed milk and chocolate, to Maidstone. The kids that stayed at home would chide those that were going with the accusing remark, *"You're afraid to stay"*. We retorted, *"You're afraid to go"*. We stayed for a short time in a house in Maidstone, near a park that had a hospital or some kind of institution in the grounds. We were put in the same bedroom where, one night, we both had nightmares - literally trying to climb the walls to escape from the confines of the place, screaming for all we were worth to gain help.

The people treated us well for the short time we were there. The teenage son took me to the park, where we caught crayfish in the fast-flowing stream that went through the centre. Once he took me to the town, where he pointed out the tall walls of Maidstone prison: I remembered my aunt Emma saying that Ted, her husband, was in there.

We were soon moved again, this time to Lenham, a small village near Maidstone. We stayed in a cottage, or farmhouse of sorts, that was in such a bad state of repair that, to get into the bedroom, I had to go through a gap in a brick wall. There wasn't any electricity; the rooms were always dark; and I cannot remember much about the house other than there being an area of cultivated cobnuts surrounded by a high, small-meshed wire netting fence preventing me from having a chance to taste them. They were bursting from their autumnal coloured cases of russet and golden brown, from which I deduced that it must have been near the end of the year. One day, during a storm, I was standing beside a fence, watching darkening clouds partially hiding the sun, when I heard distant thunder. A parting came between the clouds, allowing a bright shaft of sunlight to appear and at the same time a bird flew through the opening, turning it a bright yellow. The whole scene was startling, causing again this picture to become forever part of my consciousness. Perhaps again acting as a contrast to the dreary atmosphere the house held for me.

We were both taken to a large house in London Road, Maidstone that served as a hostel-cum-clinic for sick evacuee children. Somehow we had caught impetigo, showing as sores on our legs. We were put in a room in the front of the house, isolated because of these contagious sores. Allowed out after two weeks, I gave full vent to my pent-up energy as I caused havoc in the place. From a neighbour's garden I stole prize pears that had been trained to grow along the wall, within easy reach of my grasping hands. I climbed a fifty-foot tree with another boy and the Fire Brigade were called to get him down. Whilst the night nurse was asleep I stole sweets from the pantry, causing myself and others to be sick from eating too many. Having made bows and arrows for most of the boys, I fired an arrow across a polished table, causing another boy serious injury. I never fully realised how much damage I had done, because the nurses took me out of the room. I was also involved in the partial destruction of an old greenhouse, pulling the bricks apart, one by one, until little of the wall remained. My mother was called to take me back home, with parting words from the Matron saying that they were glad to get rid of me, as I'd been nothing but trouble since we arrived.

Home again for a short time, then herded with my sister and other children in the *Leather Bottle* pub in Belvedere to be taken to the Devon and Somerset borders. A GWR steam engine pulled the carriages, packed with children accompanied by helpers from the WVS and teachers recruited to help out on the journey. We were still carrying the name-tagged gas masks, chocolate and condensed milk. The train was exciting, travelling at such speed, blowing away my hard-held handkerchief as I waved it from the window. I really needed it to wipe the soot from my eyes, as we sped through tunnels, forgetting to close the windows. It was a journey of adventure never to be forgotten: my first experience of a corridor train.

Arriving at the school in East Anstey, on the Devon and Somerset borders, I and another boy went over the wall from the playground, waited until it was dark, then headed back to the school.

I was the last to be chosen. A tall woman asked, *"Is this one mine?"* then led me out along a darkened road, holding my hand, asking how old I was and my name, coupled with the question, 'did I like goose?' She said she had a son called John, who was my age but not as big as me. I sensed her resentment at saying I was bigger, as if it were a problem. Mrs Spencer was a very good cook and food was plentiful as Mr Spencer ran his own transport business, taking livestock around the country. Mrs Spencer also ran a taxi service from home with a small Ford car.

There were three other kids billeted in the same row as me. Dudley, Morgan, and Bowman - all older, in Mr Lee's class - came with evacuees from North Heath School. He wore rimless glasses, never smiled and seemed to carry the weight of the world on his shoulders. He once caught me in the toilets showing another boy how I could make my dick disappear into my balls to form the shape of a girl's quim. He went berserk calling me *"a filthy boy, you filthy boy, get out, get out!!"* I was quite put out by his attitude, but later, of course, associated his outburst perhaps with his religious affiliation, or his own sexually restricted upbringing.

I once again found birds intriguing, having come across a partially felled copse that exposed what I assumed to have been the nest of a buzzard, high in a fir tree made from the dead orange-coloured twigs of the fallen trees. Nearby was a chicken farm, with many *White Leghorns* roaming in a free-range area, where buzzards flew high from the reach of the farmhand's guns. I estimated there were twenty or more at any one time, though it was difficult to count because of their constant circling movements.

Seeing two Border Collies round up sheep for the first time astounded me: how they understood the farmer's command when he said, *"Gee up a round them Gyp"* in that soft Devon accent; then to watch them confine the sheep where the farmer wanted them. {*The above command is the exact one given all those years ago.}*

I had two powerful spiritual experiences when in Devon, both related to the natural world. The first and most profound was when visiting a woman, whom I believe to have been Mr Spencer's mother. We went in the car down a very narrow lane, descending into a valley where we had to stop, unable to turn left, finding it too narrow to negotiate. We had to walk the rest of the way down a steep path, eventually coming to a cottage surrounded by Beauty of Bath apple trees with much of the over- ripened fruit lying in the grass, being eaten by wasps. I was captivated by the silence and heat of the day, with the steady rhythmic buzzing sound of the wasps. Seeing the occasional butterfly, I was aware of being in the presence of a place I can only describe as sacred. Mr Spencer knocked on the door, waited for a time, then went round the back calling a name; he soon returned, saying that she was possibly elsewhere. We then walked back to the car with the deep experience contained forever in my consciousness as numinous.

I have thought about these experiences during the course of my life and attribute them to what I call my *'hidden editor'*, that something which retains those occasions like the above. It's easy to understand how a trauma or painful situation can be remembered, but what is it that grips the soul at times, imprinting forever the situations that others might dismiss as being of little consequence? Could this be Grace??

The second experience occurred when I was being taken with the class on one or other of the moors for a walk. We were told to lie down when a plane swooped low above us, not knowing if it was friend or foe. After it disappeared out of sight we were told to walk on. A few strides later, out of nowhere, at our feet, appeared a wonderful valley covered with bracken, amongst which there walked a magnificent stag with full antlers and head just visible above the high green covering. It was my first experience of such an animal and I was amazed at its beauty as it slowly walked with head held high in such grandeur. It was such a contrast with the threat of the war machine that had passed over us all, moments beforehand, making such a frightening noise. To have the stillness and silence coupled with the sighting of the stag was another experience which is forever etched, indelibly, in my memory.

I was the only evacuee in Miss Brown's class: forever playing up; taking in very little other than frequent doses of the stick that often broke on impact with my now nine-year-old outstretched hand. Miss Brown had grey hair with the look of someone in her sixties, and would no doubt find these sticks lying on the ground when walking in the woods. They were consequently very dry, or partially rotten, causing them to break, which evoked laughter from everyone, including me - much to her annoyance.

One day, Mr Lee combined the two classes and drew three squares on the blackboard, explaining that they represented three fields: one containing chickens, one a fox, and one a dangerous bull. He then asked how the farmer went from a- to- b without having to go through the field which contained the bull. I immediately saw the answer and gave it. Mr Lee very curtly dismissed my answer saying, *"Yes, that's right Farquhar"* without a *"very, well done my lad"*. I instinctively deduced I had upset him by getting the answer right, but in some perverse way had avenged the incident in the toilets, when he made such a fuss of my action – a fuss I considered unwarranted.

Mrs Spencer would tell her neighbours that my mother didn't send her any money for my new shoes and boots, both of which I wore out quickly. My mother came eventually but I didn't see her, for such a row broke out between the two women, with my mother getting too much of the truth from the church going, respectable Spencers. I was later told that my mother was wearing a fur coat and looked like a prostitute. Mrs Spencer had alluded to the fact that her coat had cost a lot of money but couldn't send enough for my clothes. I didn't know the meaning of the word 'prostitute'.

I recall two winters at the school because of the slides we built on the hard-packed snow, made by the constant polishing of the smooth-soled boots of the slide enthusiasts. Anyone found sliding without the proper footwear was soon sent packing, for it was with a sense of pride that we protected the glass smooth surface. Once, during a snowball fight, Morgan hit me with a particularly hard one that had a piece of ice inside. The thing hurt me, and I was even more incensed at seeing Morgan smiling at his ploy, thinking what a good trick he had performed. My ear was still stinging when I went for him, raining blows on his not so happy face, as I landed some well-directed punches. I never had any more trouble from him, or Dudley, or Bowman. They eventually stole my knife before I returned home, by making out they had dropped it amongst grass, when running along some high ground near where we lived.

One Sunday morning, sitting in my room, I heard the Spencers tickling John as they all laughed loudly. I felt an overwhelming loneliness break through the tough exterior I had learnt to live behind. Tears fell from my cheeks for the first time in my life and I couldn't understand the reason.

The other three didn't play with me after stealing my knife, so I was mostly on my own. A shop had closed in the village and I found packets of seeds abandoned in the garden. I took some to sow, intending to make a garden in a field with a spring in it. I had expectations of having my own flowered area in the field, but it wasn't to be - my mother came for me and I was taken back home. Arriving back that first night, I heard someone I thought was my father speaking to my mother in their bedroom. I went off to sleep knowing I would see my father in the morning. When I woke I asked my mother where my father was, as I thought I had heard him in the night, but she said I must have been dreaming and that he had not been there. Her reply was like a stab wound to me, knowing that she was with someone else, deceiving my father and the whole family. She'd lied!! She'd lied!! The words echoed through my body, affecting me like some insidious poison. I wasn't dreaming, I wasn't, and she had been with someone else while my father was away! What should have been a homecoming filled with elation and joy turned into utter confusion and despair. The burden of being part of this adult world was suddenly placed on my young shoulders, leaving me with such deep feelings of hatred toward my mother. In that black and white mindset of hate attributed to my young mind, it had a lasting affect on me.

A few days later my mother's youngest sister Kathy, who was born only three months after me, came to visit us. She had heard Granny say that my mother had a name around Erith like a *'Greyhound'*, meaning that everyone knew her to be the local whore, frequenting the pubs of the town for a good time while her husband was away in the army. This confirmed what I had already guessed. I said *"Yes, Kathy. I know!"*

I returned to the infants at North Heath, aware of being behind in most subjects but especially in arithmetic. One incident of import occurred on my first day back in the school, when the young teacher said, *"I have to give you this lesson, so you can make of it what you like. I do not believe in it; it's up to you"*. He then read one of the scriptures and something from the Bible. I thought, with my childish logic, that if a man like this cannot understand or believe it, how can I, a mere boy, expect to either? So from that day on I dismissed God and miracles as bunk: not to be afraid of God looking down on me from high. Soon after this lesson I met a new friend who taught me to masturbate during those difficult introverted times.

War Years in Erith

I heard Clare Rayner on the radio say how the song of the '*Jolly Miller*' reflected the way she felt as a child. I, coincidentally, had the same association with that song. The words, "*I care for nobody, no not I, for nobody cares for me*" rang true, describing the way I felt when at my lowest ebb, dismissing the occasional thoughts of taking my own life. My sister Barbara was in Devon; my brother John in the north of England with a kind family who adored him. Bobby was home with me, too young to be affected by the actions of my mother at this stage of the war.

My mother was friendly with the local Pilot, who knew which ships were due to be berthed at Erith. The names of the ships had a special meaning to the women who visited our house: they would get excited when they learned which ships were due, with their fancy men, as they called them, on board. My mother would often mispronounce the ships' names, so I sometimes had to guess which one she meant. One in particular was called the '*Handifoam*' or '*Handifone*'; another the '*Empire Hearth*'.

The pilot was a dirty fellow: he wore a grubby mackintosh that matched the colour of his teeth and the bicycle he rode. He was quite often there in the afternoons when I came home from school, bringing with him a variety of basic foodstuffs - margarine, sultanas and the like, in fact anything he could scrounge from the ships' cooks - so we were never short of food, as my mother could bake anything. Cooking was her way of expressing her love for us. Being the eldest of nine, she had rarely received the intimacy she must have craved as a child.

Our schooling was disrupted around this time, as we had to attend the homes of various teachers for lessons. The head, Mr Ancel, lived in Parsonage Manor Way. I recall going to his home and to other teachers' homes close by.

This was the quiet period during the war, when air raids were few. I was now in my tenth year, and we were all glad to be together in our family home. Once, when we were all sitting around the table finishing a meal, my mother chided me about something petty, in a jocular manner, whilst the others joined in with a mantra-like chant directed towards me - all in good fun, but somehow I couldn't handle what was happening. Feeling I was being ridiculed, I just flipped, and flew into a rage. I went for my mother with a broken milk bottle that I smashed on the brass fender placed around the hearth, holding it in my hand and screaming at her to stop. I was shaking with anger at feeling that I had been ridiculed, holding the jagged end of the bottle in my hand, threatening her with it if she didn't stop. Taken aback at my outburst, my mother placated me with condescending language like, *"All right Ronnie … it won't happen anymore … put*

41

the bottle away ... come and sit down with us at the table ... I will clear the mess up". The bottle had had milk in it before I picked it up so, when I smashed it on the fender, milk went all over the floor and fireplace.

Although only ten, I could not take the concerted ridicule of the family, and being the eldest I felt I had taken on the role of a surrogate father to my younger siblings. This, coupled with the anger I felt over my mother's actions with men and the reputation she had gained, must have been subconsciously festering within me, waiting for release. I could not forgive her actions nor control the feeling of injustice I had to bare.

When the raids became more frequent, our mother would still visit the pubs in Erith to pick up men. The favourites were the *Cross Keys*, the *Wheatley Arms*, and the *Plough* – as well as others along the way when they felt like a change. These were the most often spoken about when they dressed up for a night on the town. There would also be the occasional party, which meant I would get the deposit money left on the beer bottles when I returned them to the pub the next day. I would often be kept awake by the partying, so I went to school very tired. Indeed, on one occasion I felt so tired that I fell off the edge of the kerb as I awoke. I had slept as I walked!

When the raids were on, we had to leave the comfort of bed to go into the shelter. This was made worse by a mobile gun placed at the top of our road, some sixty feet away, which created a hell of a noise. Occasionally I would look out from the bedroom windows to see the sky lit up with searchlights, picking out German bombers as they flew towards London.

Our neighbour, Mr Partridge, would ask if we were all right as we entered the shelter. I would lie and say in reply that everything was OK, putting on a brave face to reassure the others, making out that all was well as we went into that musty-smelling place of safety. We all huddled into a damp makeshift bed and waited for the bombs to stop; the siren to sound the '*all clear*'. Then back to the house again, into the clean-smelling bedroom. At the time we all shared the large bed in the big room in the front of the house. The room had black curtains to make it completely dark, so the Germans couldn't see our lights and then bomb us: we did as we were told in the Ministry Of Information films shown in the local cinemas.

I would lie awake in the night, watching the reflections of headlights of various vehicles travelling along Colyers Lane, intrigued at how this was possible, since all vehicles had to have covers over their headlights to deflect the beams to the ground. But somehow the reflection would still enter through a gap at the top of the curtains, allowing the light to run round the frieze on our bedroom ceiling. I never did fathom out how this occurred: it kept me guessing for a long time. Masturbation was a form of enjoyment, of course, that would help me to pass the time when the others were asleep in that darkened room.

Our favourite pastime during the dark winter nights was listening to the radio, or 'wireless' as it was then known. 'ITMA' was one of the best, coupled with 'Monday Night at Eight o' Clock' and, of course, 'Appointment with Fear'. This programme would frighten us so badly we would be too scared to go to the loo, unless armed with a weapon to protect ourselves, such as a poker from the fireplace. Visits from one of my mother's circle, an Irish friend, gave us endless pleasure, listening to the way she pronounced the days of the week.

Mother bought me a large sheath knife, after continuous pleading, as most kids had them. It was a fad at the time to have one, mainly for throwing into trees. I would practise most of the night, making deep indents in the doors: they all suffered this abuse from my constant pounding with the knife. One door in particular, in the front room, was most affected by my compulsive throwing. This was the one my mother hung her best coat from: I would try to get as near to the arm as possible. Sometimes I would pin the arm to the door as I missed the target, but it would not bother me: it acted as a release for my pent-up anger. That would be unconsciously sated as I threw the knife. My mother must have seen the holes where the sleeve had been pierced, but never mentioned them to me. This destructive behaviour held no bounds, as I used my catapult during the day to kill birds, break windows or break the white china cones on telegraph poles.

I would often break the window in the front door to get into the house if I found the door locked. Breaking anything would produce in me a sense of joy. I do remember having qualms when I destroyed a sunflower on an allotment. It broke halfway down the stem when I hit it with full force on the flower head. It was the limp state in which I left it that stuck in my mind, coupled with the knowledge it had been tended by someone, who used the seed to feed a caged bird. Seed was hard to get during the war.

Another time, my conscience pricked me as I smashed a weather vane high on top of a pole. It was in a garden, made from wood in the shape of a small house. This was another target for my catapult but again I felt bad, knowing someone had tenderly constructed it. The clock on the church steeple at Erith came under concerted attack from us on one occasion, as we succeeded in breaking sections of glass on the face.

This change of character was something to ponder: from a boy who could be moved so passionately by a bird's nest with five blue eggs, to someone who 4 years later would, without compunction, kill birds and threaten to attack his mother with a broken bottle. Looking back now, I can associate easily with Hamlet in my plight, having a mother who deceived his father. Some years later a Probation Officer was to say of my mother, *"She is a good mother but a bad wife."* It was the beginning of evil entering my life, spreading within my consciousness, leading to hate and a disturbed psyche that would lead me to self-destructive behaviour. Some of my other siblings did the same.

Neither my brothers nor my sister ever fully recovered from the effects of our experiences. Although being left home alone during the air raids did profound harm to us all, we found separate ways to cope and develop inner resilience. I had a good voice and copied Diana Durbin with a high soprano trill. Our neighbour, Mrs Partridge, would comment on this to my mother. I liked to sing and was also attracted to classical music, which I would conduct with an imaginary baton as I stood in front of the wireless.

Once, while waiting for my friend to finish his violin lesson, I rested my head on the door jamb and then went into a trance-like state, aware of a violin concerto that was repeated a few times. His opening the door woke me up, and I asked if he had finished the two hours: he replied that he had. To me it was only a few minutes: the time had somehow been compressed. It has forever been a mystery. I later learned it was Tchaikovsky's Violin Concerto.

My uncle Bert would occasionally call round with a friend, asking my mother to buy articles he had stolen. Once, when I came home from school, I found my

Grandfather Bert and some other men in the bathroom, whispering as they busily involved themselves with - something. There was an air of excitement: the sound of muffled voices and the sound of tools rattling. I later learned that my mother's cousin from Edmonton had escaped from a coach when in transit from court to a prison in Kent. The commotion was caused by their cutting off his handcuffs with a hacksaw. His name was Israel Small and he'd kicked his way out of the coach window, then been picked up by an accomplice in a car and driven to our house for the cuffs to be removed.

My father occasionally came home on leave from the south coast where he was manning artillery and searchlight batteries. I recall him coming home with a kitbag full of articles he had stolen from houses that had been evacuated – left empty because shells fired from France were landing in that area. On one occasion he dug a hole in the garden to bury antique clocks wrapped in sacking. This was for a short time until he could sell them. They were far too expensive for us to have: we would have been arrested immediately.

My mother was always in a good mood when an opportunity to get extra money came her way - she could always find willing buyers for good quality items. Bert would steal furniture from the Rex cinema, stored there from houses that had been bombed. To the average crook this would be the lowest act of all, stealing from those who might one day return to look for their possessions. Bert and his friends had no problem with this: it was an easy option to take the small stuff, left unguarded in a place like a cinema - he didn't have any conscience about it at all. Perhaps coming from the anti-social background he experienced contributed to a lack of conscience for his actions.

Our neighbour, Mrs Partridge, put comics through the letterbox for me - the Wizard, Beano and Hotspur. I enjoyed reading them, though they were really intended for her son, Tommy, who was eighteen and serving in the Tank Regiment: she said I could have them until he came back. Tragically, he was killed on the day before the war ended, by a direct hit from a German anti-tank gun. I always felt grateful for this gesture that later led me to library books. Tommy comes to mind each year on Remembrance Sunday, for his contribution to my life, bless him.

The cinemas at Erith were a good source of escape from the war, my mother and her friends. The Warner Brothers films, shown at the Odeon Cinema, interested me most, because I liked the sound tracks of Max Steiner, Leo F Forbstein, Franz Waxman - composers who captured my interest when reading the credits. It was great watching the *'Dead End Kids'* with Mugs McGuinness, the gang leader who often took his hat off to hit the droopy fellow. There were war films like *'Back to Battan'* and *'Guadalcanal Diary'*, showing

48

the Americans being killed by the sneaky Japs who did the dirtiest of tricks, such as pretending to give themselves up then turn the tables on the righteous Yanks by shooting them when their backs were turned. All good propaganda stuff that we kids would boo, too, sitting in the comfort of warm cinema seats.

The Ritz was the cheaper of the two and the best for a Sunday get together with the local crowd. This included Rickets, my main helper when it came to making catapults under my direction. We were the best shots and competed with each other to kill birds or smash bottles on the local council dump at Barnhurst.

We played in the large gardens of the empty houses in the better off areas of Erith. Once inside, stealing books was a favourite way to spend our time. We would take anything that suited us, such as fruit when in abundance at the right time of the year. Sometimes we would saw or chop down a tree just for the fun of it, paint the walls of empty houses for revenge when the owners ran off until war was over. That's what they got for leaving - walls daubed with Swastikas, the German emblem, in black paint.

After a raid, we would look in the field at the back of the house to see if we could find any live incendiary bombs. They would be about two feet deep in the soft earth and we used a hooked piece of iron rod to catch onto the fin. Then we would pull out the whole bomb (it was about two feet long and two inches in diameter), unscrew the detonator, put a nail in, place it at the bottom of a tree, climb around six feet high then drop a brick on it making it explode - our form of wartime firework.

Eventually the Germans dropped anti-personnel devices called butterfly bombs: they had a wing-shaped attachment which allowed them to get caught up in trees. The Ministry of Information films shown in all the local cinemas gave good warning about these bombs, but a local fellow unfortunately did touch one and was badly injured, losing an eye as part of his wounds. His name was Bob Grasby. I mention this involvement with the incendiary bombs because it was an attitude I had cultivated, no doubt stemming from my need to destroy, which had become so much a part of my nature.

The Seniors School

Now in my eleventh year, I had to go to the Senior School in Brook Street, next to the Infants. On the first day I had a fight with another boy who thought he would bully me in front of his pals, as perhaps he had been bullied a year earlier. We exchanged a few punches, then there was a stand-off, both eyeing each other waiting to make a move. By now we had found ourselves in the toilets, surrounded by a baying crowd egging us on to fight. I had one of his cronies, with his face about a foot from mine, jeering me to continue, calling me names. I landed a good punch, right on his nose, making the blood spurt over the white urinal wall, just as the water was flushing down, giving a bloody curtain of rivulets, as it ran away into the gully. By now my opponent had disappeared, as the bell went for the playtime to finish. I was never bothered again: in fact I had a reputation as someone not to mess with when it came to fighting. The blood in the urinal helped - looking very effective at the right time.

From the first day at North Heath Secondary Modern I couldn't wait to leave and make my way in the world. I was in the lowest of forms (the D's) to start with, then up to the C's. I couldn't master Arithmetic so I helped Rickets with English: he did arithmetic for me. With this simple arrangement I managed to hide my innumeracy for the whole time I was at that school.

Raids were now few, except for sneak raiders who would get through undetected by our (by then primitive) radar defences. I saw handcarts that had been used by *Grooms* the bakers, with holes in them made by machine gun fire. How the fellows who were pulling or pushing them fared, I do not know, but the damage was there to be seen.

The American dump was a favourite place for us to go. We would wait for the jeep to arrive each morning with the rubbish, driven by soldiers dressed in dull 'fatigue' clothes denoting punishment duties. They tipped the bins in a special place away from the council area. It arrived every day at half past ten to discharge the goodies for us to rummage amongst: half-filled packets of Lucky Strikes, Chesterfields, Camels, and Kools cigarettes, a special favourite not seen in England that had a menthol taste, plus many packets of condoms that sometimes contained a small sheet of paper, showing a soldier and a girl against a tree, doing what comes naturally. Then another picture showing the same soldier lying on a hospital bed, with two captions explaining his plight: *'A Little Bit of This' Can Lead to a Lot of That*. He didn't look a happy bunny.

We had to bunk off school to get these things. We would find lots of gum, sweets, watches and magazines, the best of which were *'Life'* and *'Picture Post'*. Once I arranged with the others of the gang to hang condoms along the avenue of trees from the main gates to the school. We urinated in some for added effect. In the morning assembly the head was not amused, for sex in those days was still a taboo subject. He said, *"Would the culprits not hang the balloons along the drive again"*. We all had a laugh at his expense, knowing how embarrassed they would all be, making their way along the drive with such strange fruits of war hanging limp along the way.

We busied ourselves by making use of the cinemas, woods, bombed houses and those left empty by the rich, where I found books. One was *'The Man Eaters Of Tsavo'*, a true story about the laying of the railway line through Africa, where lions took many of the Indian labourers into the bush. One of the largest they killed measured nine feet from the nose to the end of the tail. I later heard it mentioned on a radio programme, called *'Old Books and New'* – I was elated at having read the book mentioned.

We were always getting involved in some scrape or other, but the crunch came when Harvey was caught stealing charity boxes from shop counters. He told the police we had benefited from his exploits, that he had given some of the money to us, and to some extent this was true, but I only had some of the proceeds from one box. The court decided that we were all guilty and each parent accused the other's child of being the culprit, responsible for their sons having a police record.

We each had a reason for our actions. Harvey's parents worked too bloody hard running a lodging house and taxi service. Richards came from a large family with an alcoholic father who was a river lighterman and rarely at home. We were all given probation for two years, to attend Dartford Probation Service. I got on well with the Probation Officer, Mr Coles, a short tubby fellow who suggested I join the 'Army Cadets,' which I did later.

One day a prefect called to take me to the head's office - I quickly deduced what he would want me for. Realising I had cigarettes and a lighter in my pockets, I told the fellow to wait for me while I went to the toilet. I took quite a time hiding the articles, and when the head came in he caught me red handed hiding the cache in the last toilet along the row. Holding me by the ear, he marched me to the office where the Caretaker, a Mr Grix, was seated. He showed surprise at the head bringing in a suspect offender.

"So what have you got to say for yourself now?" blurted out the now elated head, after catching me so easily, showing his prize to Mr Grix. The head was now walking around me, confident at having caught me so easily. Standing in front of his desk he said, *"Mr Grix, Farquhar has found twenty Players cigarettes in the toilets where boys have been smoking. Do you know any boys that have been smoking there, Farquhar?"* I replied that I didn't know of any boys smoking there. He then countered, *"Mr Grix has seen*

boys smoking there". I foolishly asked *"when Sir?"* whereupon he grabbed the cane from the desk, held me over his half-bended knee … and shouting in temper said *"I'm asking the questions lad!!"*

He gave me six hard cuts of the cane on my bare legs. As he did so I saw Grix wince at every blow, as he beat down on me with full force, making searing marks on my legs. I was told to get back to the class; the lighter and cigarettes were confiscated. It was the first time in my life I had been so badly hurt physically by another person. But it did me a lot of good. I didn't wish to have another dose of the treatment so I knuckled down, taking a keener interest in the lessons, staying clear of trouble more or less until I left.

Both Vallis and I would have our work read to the class as examples of description. On one occasion the teacher 'Bookie Read' called me to his desk, asking if the word 'mystifying' would sound better in a sentence I had written. He suggested it should replace the word 'mystic' in the sentence *'The black water of the moat stood in silent mystic stillness'*. I declined his suggestion; he allowed it to stay; which I thought was good of him - me a mere boy. How did this word come to my eleven-year-old vocabulary? I had no recollection of ever reading the meaning of it. Once again, I can only ascribe this episode, along with others I was to have, as being attributed to my 'hidden editor', as being an act of Grace which I was to have as an added portent in later life.

There were times when my mother was under a lot of stress through our father stopping one or both of her allowances. He did this because of her actions, as a way of getting something over her. She spoke of her plight to friends, coupled with details of the diseases she had. They argued over who was to blame for their sexual infections.

To help with money she contracted to do the washing for the ships kitchens: this was arranged between the pilots. She used the washing lines of three or more neighbours and by the time she had finished she was exhausted. I'd never seen her so tired, doing it all by hand because of my father stopping the money. She eventually found work cooking in a Civic Restaurant in Northumberland Heath. This made all the difference to our money problems, for she occasionally took food from there, hidden in her bag. We also bought cheap meals there with others who were finding it difficult coping on the rations allowed.

Although money was short as a consequence of my father's frequently stopping it, we were never short of food, for I believe my mother had two sets of ration books, making out she'd lost the originals. When fruit was available from the gardens of empty houses, she would make small tarts which we sold to neighbours; at Christmas time we made paper flowers that I sold in Bexleyheath Broadway. My grandmother collected teasels from the marshes and coloured them with bright clothing dyes to sell in Watney Street Market in the East End. The relative who was known as the 'Heron' made wonderful chrysanthemums from the wood of the elderberry by cutting with a sharp knife to form the bloomed head. She would then dye them various colours after placing them on a straight willow stem.

A time came when the problems of living were too much for mother and she thought it easier to end it all. One night she put us all into her bed in the front of the house. I heard the money being put in the gas meter, realising what she had planned, so I repeated to myself '*don't fall asleep*', '*I cannot fall asleep*'. I would have died along with my brothers and sister had I fallen asleep. I knew I had to stay awake, to save us all by opening the windows that were tightly closed, since I, being the nearest to the gas fire, would be first to go. I was moving around for a long time, trying hard not to sleep, when my mother spoke from outside the room, beside the open door, and told me I could go back to my bed. With hindsight, she must have been waiting for us all to go to sleep then to lie down with us to end it all. I was the only one aware of this harrowing incident.

Whether we would all have perished that night is open to doubt - it was a big room and it would have taken a lot of gas to accomplish her aim. However, if any of us had put on the light switch the whole top floor would have been blown up. Reports were frequent of gas-filled rooms being ignited by turning the light on: the spark from the switch would have been enough to cause it to explode.

Hop Picking

I was around twelve when I went hop picking with my grandmother and aunts Emma and Mary to Marden in Kent. It was the occasion of the year, looked on as a working holiday where you could let your hair down and, if single, find yourself a hopping (mush or moult). A lot was made of these days away; the weather was always good, I was told. Amongst those going, there was an air of excitement - anticipation of earning good money whilst at the same time taking a break from their uneventful lives. A lorry was hired amongst, say, six families. They all piled in with the most important item of all, the pram that held the majority of the things needed, including bedding, crockery, clothing and food - not forgetting the large pot needed for cooking on the open fire, plus the other requisite saucepans and water containers.

We arrived late in the afternoon, eager to get to the huts, fix up the place ready for the night, and get the fire started with the faggots the farmer supplied. Walking from the lorry with the prams was an event in itself, pushing the prams through deep grass, disturbing thousands of crane flies that September day. Excited exchanges could be heard as we pushed through the grass, like, "Isn't it ***cushty to be back here … my Emma ready to earn a few poaches again … ****dick eye, the **dinlo mush with the *chavvies over there my Mary". All heads would be

59

turned towards a man struggling with his children and pram crossing the field, no doubt making heavy weather of it.

*Children
** Madman
*** Good
**** To look at

It wasn't long before my grandmother would have the fire roaring and the kettle boiling, soon ready for the tea. Kath and I had collected the water and wood faggots before they all disappeared. We always operated together, looking for empty milk bottles that we would get the return money on, scrumping apples to make tarts, collecting blackberries, and shopping every day for food. I was very conscious how much I ate, so I worked hard all day on the bin, picking the hops for my grandmother.   It taught me patience, having to stay by the stall all day picking into an old enamel bowl and then, when full, transferring it into the large bin.

It was here that I saw my first fight between two men. Seeing the savagery of it scared me so much I walked away, fearing to watch. It seemed to have been over a woman: a woman's name was mentioned as they screamed obscenities at each other while they kicked and punched as if in a fight to the death. There seemed to be a lot of blood as I took my last backward look at them.

Most weekends, a drunken gypsy rode his pony and trap between the rows of huts, at the same time running his whip along the corrugated iron roofs, making a hell of a din. As the cart knocked over whatever was foolishly left in his path, he swore as he went, cursing the world and all that he thought was wrong with it. He was in his fifties, big built, wearing a trilby hat that never came off, even as the trap swerved in all directions as it went on its crazy way. He enjoyed himself, being such a bloody nuisance, and far too fast for anyone to stop him.

There were occasional rows and sometimes fights over horses between the Bevin Boys and gypsies. The 'Bevin Boys' were young men not fit enough for the Services but needed for filling in where able bodied men were wanted for strenuous work, like working on the land and the mines, in effect taking the place of others called up in the forces. I never saw the fights but only became aware of them from rumours around the camp. Sometimes girls would be the cause of upset between the two factions, as the travelling girls were exceptionally good looking, willing to cause trouble and flirt. The first week, there was a strike over the amount paid for a bushel of hops, but it was soon resolved after a day or two without any picking. Then back to normal, with mainly glorious sunshine away from the horrors of the raids or news of the war: for we had no any way of knowing what was happening back home.

My first experience of hopping had been full of excitement and I looked forward to the following year.

I was still doing well at school in my twelfth year, but concerned by my mother's actions, and my father was still coming home trying to catch her with other men. We were awakened late one night by the sound of our father holding a very frightened man around the neck in an arm lock saying, *"This is what your mother is getting up to while I am away."* I had mixed feelings about what was happening because, in one way, I was sorry for the plight of the man, but glad my mother had been found out at last with a man in the act of sleeping with her, thankfully still wearing his clothes.

We were all scared about the outcome, although it was over in a few minutes. We nestled down to sleep again, glad to have some peace - each with our own thoughts. Where did the man go? Did our father kill him and such like? Not the ideal homecoming for a child to sleep on.

About this time I had an interest in collecting birds' eggs and saving cigarette cards, a hobby initiated by a gift from my aunt Joan, my father's youngest sister. The cards were in a wonderful condition, each set bound by elastic bands as good as the day they were made. I was proud to have them for they far surpassed any of my friends' collections. I also found books in her house that interested me: bound with blue Morocco leather they were called '*A Wonderland of Knowledge'.* I enjoyed the times I spent in the house: it was so clean and on occasion I received money for the pictures. My maternal grandmother's home had a loving feeling: I certainly felt more cared for with them, because I always had food and felt part of the family.

Learning About Sex;

The Man in the Homburg Hat

During my twelfth year, sex made its way into my life in the form of abuse by others. One concerned an older boy in the road, who used me by putting his dick between my legs until near ejaculation, then finishing the rest himself. I felt no particular shame of abuse at the time, for being naive about an act of this kind I thought it as natural as helping someone, say, in tying a parcel and being asked to put my finger on the knot while they tied the string. It happened on two occasions in the toilet of our house.

The other incident was more serious. It occurred when another older boy asked if I would like to go for a ride in a car with a family friend. I agreed to go with them one night. It was my first ride, so not to be missed, as few people had cars in those days. I went with them and, as soon as we stopped, he came round the back, got down on his knees, undid my fly then started to suck my dick. I was so shocked I couldn't do anything. Afraid to move, I willed myself not to respond to what he was doing. I was terrified and embarrassed at the same time so willing with all my mental control, I forced my body not to feel pleasure from the actions of this man. After about five minutes he ceased, upset at not having achieved his desired end, and gave me a half a crown. The fellow who had taken me to him sat on the seat at the back, watching all that went on. He was a couple of years older than me. I was afraid that I could have been murdered: such was my level of fear as it was taking place.

Some weeks later, as I was sitting on the pan in the toilets opposite the town hall, I noticed a pencil protrude from a hole in the door, after forcing a piece of paper out. I soon finished what I was doing and then looked through the hole, only to see a brown eye on the other side, a quarter of an inch away, looking at mine. I shot back in panic, turning my back to the door, and waited until someone else came to use the place. I didn't have to wait long before a bus conductor bounded down the steps, with money and keys rattling in his bag. I took my chance and went out. As I looked to my left I saw the man with the Homburg hat using the corner urinal. I was glad to get away from him.

Sometime later, when I was with friends – all armed with our catapults - we saw the fellow again, loitering outside the same loos. I had previously told the others about what had happened with him in the car, so we fired stones at him from a distance and ran away. I am sure I saw him dance around, as one of the shots hit him on the ankle. It was the last time I ever saw him.

It would have been easier for me to omit these episodes of sexual abuse but, in my aim for the truth in this account of my life, I want to express the importance of the psychological as well as the social relevance.

The bodies of two evacuee brothers were found trussed and murdered in a cupboard, somewhere in Devonshire, at the end of the war. The find caused a public outcry at the sheer horror of it. They were known as the 'Gough Brothers'. Without the benefit of a stable background, I and others like me were open to abuse from predatory perverts who were only too aware of the weakness in the characters of psychologically abused kids.

The war was now coming to an end, to our advantage, with the Russian advance routing the German Sixth Army under General Von Paulus. I once saw a picture in a paper of a frozen German soldier, giving the '*Heil Hitler*' salute with his outstretched hand pointing to the sky, in his last act of defiance and loyalty to the Third Reich.

One night, during a heavy raid, after taking the others to the shelter, I was looking from the back bedroom window at the dog fights taking place. As I watched the spectacle, deeply involved with my grandstand view, my father came into the room, asking if our mother was out. I replied, "*Out as usual*". I was glad to have my father at home beside me, watching the scene before us, enjoying the intimacy of being together. My father made an observation about the speed of one of the planes that had flames coming from its tail. In the morning it was confirmed to be a new weapon: a Flying Bomb. Soon there were many of these being dropped around us, causing much damage. There was one in particular which I shall refer to later.

The boy who assaulted me in the toilet took me to Dartford to pick up girls. He was about three years older than me, with dark, curly hair that attracted the girls .The format when in Dartford would be to walk round the square in pairs, then bump into any girls that where going in the opposite direction. It would be completely dark and quite a bit of groping would ensue, coupled with a lot of giggling as others behind would push forward, splitting up the first group. Then it all started again with other couples.

Sometimes we would bring small torches and shine them in the face of a girl we'd bumped into. On odd occasions they wouldn't mind roving hands rubbing their breasts. This was Dartford after dark, a place where teenagers would meet any evening, safe in the knowledge that the war was ending and that raids were therefore less frequent. Some would wear luminous badges to prevent others colliding with them.

My friend was adept at picking up girls: anything would suit him, ugly or otherwise. I would go with their mates just to keep him company. I was well out of my depth at these meetings, not finding the experience very helpful as I was so young. This friend had many girl friends, including a married woman whose husband was in the forces. She was twenty nine and lived in Doris Avenue, North Heath. I was with him one day at her house when she called for him to come into bed with her. I felt as though I was in the way and left, leaving them both to it.

There were more Flying Bombs dropping around the district, causing a lot of damage. I recently read about this in the press, because the double agent, Eddie Chapman, fed wrong information to the Germans, making the bombs fall short - hitting central London. In consequence, there were fewer air raids to keep us awake at night.

My mother and her friends had switched their interest to the pubs in Woolwich, picking up soldiers back on leave from the front, with plenty of money to spend: easy pickings for the astute whores wanting a good time for nothing.

I was now thirteen and reaching puberty, with a lot happening to me: I had long trousers with a new blue serge suit and I began to take an interest in my appearance. I was interested in fashion, my voice broke, of course, and I had my first sexual experience.

My mother had taken up with a soldier called Sam who was very good to us. He would help me sell the waxed flowers we made from crepe paper. He would do anything for her, being completely besotted. Sam was home with us most of the time, doing whatever he could around the house. He had quite a lot of booty that he had taken from occupied countries and prisoners, particularly things like watches and binoculars that my mother either sold or pawned. We all liked Sam for his kindness.

Our father had been transferred to the Channel Islands, guarding German prisoners. He would write, telling me how the Germans thought he was such a good fellow, because he was so big, with such strong arms. This was what German girls liked about a man, being such a good looking fellow. In one letter he said that when he had to get in the lorry, he handed his rifle up to them first. They were such great chaps, he would write, and they were teaching him German. My father was very vain and would fall for any form of flattery - they must have found him amusing. After a time, Sam either went off to a new posting or back to his own family in the north of England. We all missed him when he went.

We were still getting the flying bombs that we now called doodlebugs. One hot night, I was playing cricket with some friends in the field in front of the house. The siren went, warning us to go to the shelters, but as I was next to bat I cajoled two other fellows to continue the game. After about ten minutes, the drone of a bomb could be heard coming, then into view over the roof–tops, coming towards us. We all ran towards the gaps in the fence. I made it to the houses where I curled up as small as I could, placing a hand over each ear then closing my mouth tight.

I kept still, half listening to the thing when the engines cut off as it ran out of fuel, then a loud whistle before the almighty explosion that blew me along the passage of the house I had huddled beside. I was covered in dust and pieces of glass that came from the small panes in the door. I picked myself up, ran into the road, eager to see where the bomb had landed. The two other players were in the road shaking with shock and crying. I felt excited; eager to see what damage had been done; and ran off in the direction of Hurst Road. I was there in a few minutes and saw a gas main burning, giving a jet of flame around seven feet from the bottom of a crater the size of an average car. About me were the auxiliary services, attending to the wounded and giving out tea to those in shock; some had red blankets around them. One small, grey-haired man was sitting on the wall with a blanket over his shoulders, smoking a cigarette that had been given to him by a fireman. His face was badly bloodied by glass shards and soon the cigarette was as red as his face from the blood running down it. In the area of impact there were only parts of houses standing, with beds hanging from what was left of rooms. Dead pets lay in the road, badly gashed as the impact of the blast had thrown them against hard objects. It was said that this type of bomb exploded outwards, making a very shallow crater: the conventional bomb made a deeper crater exploding upwards, in effect lessening the blast.

I had seen the power of the bomb that day, knowing that just one hundred yards further down the road a stick of three five-hundred-pounders had been dropped some months before in Colyers Lane. I looked for the wicket, bat, and balls from our exciting game, but they had disappeared: the bomb had dropped just two hundred yards from where we had been playing.

My parents eventually separated. I was the main witness to my mother's adultery with her favourite boyfriend at the time, a soldier called Lofty from the barracks in Woolwich. I had to tell the court how she had slept with him on a specific occasion, mentioning the fact that they were in bed together. My mother and her sister Margie tried to prevent me being a witness by saying my father was a homosexual, basing this on what happened to my brother John when he was an evacuee. My mother said to me that the woman John lodged with became suspicious after my father had visited him. Was this woman covering for her older son by saying this?

I was still living at home with my mother when the court proceedings were going through, yet my father and his solicitor persuaded me to give evidence in court. I was aware of my father's promiscuity, because my mother often mentioned how stupid she had been in the past when he would lie to her, saying he was going to a Trade Union Meeting, dressed in his best suit to meet other women. She justified her own actions on the basis of his past deceit. I felt a little guilty in court, openly vilifying her in public and seeing her at last judged for her actions.

I eventually took the advice of the Probation Officer and joined the Army Cadets, along with other boys in the road: after a time I even came to enjoy it. I was now friendly with another lad of my age whose mother was called the painted doll because of her heavy make-up. Girls were our only interest now and one night when walking through a narrow pathway we met two girls heading towards us. After a few acts of flirting, by preventing them from passing, we kissed them quite spontaneously in mutual innocence then walked away in the opposite direction feeling the world owed us nothing - happy to have acted with those girls in mutual affection on the spur of the moment, coupled with an adolescent urge to embrace the opposite sex.

The war ended in Europe and I went hop-picking again with my grandmother, Kath, Emma, Margie and Mary. Everything was going well until the whole camp went down with severe stomach problems which turned to dysentery. My grandmother devised a drink from blackberry leaves and roots that acted very quickly. You boiled it first then drank it cold. It was very bitter but it did the trick, and the whole camp soon returned to work. She should have been rewarded for her knowledge of natural hedgerow remedies. Kathy and I still did the shopping and water-carrying, getting the wood and faggots of thin twigs that the farmer left once a week. One day, when we were away shopping in the village of Goudhurst, we missed a fight between our family and another from the East End of London. Prior to going to Goudhurst, Kathy had been cleaning her shoes, when a small piece of mud she flicked off with a stick had accidentally struck one of the young teenage girls, who was part of this East End family. It appeared that all members from both families became involved and from what I gathered the other family quickly learnt it didn't pay to take on a travelling family in a fight, especially one that had to live the way they had on the Marsh. My aunt Emma had lost an eye as a child, when my grandmother threw a fork at her for not doing as she was told while waiting for dinner. She was the most aggressive of them all: it was said she fought like a man. Having a glass eye as a child didn't help in the tough environment they had to live in. My aunt Marge never forgot that day, often referring to it whenever we met in later years, expressing how she had punched her opponent, *up the lips, and nose, making it all a gore of blood*. It had been the highlight of her life, apart from her marriage and children.

My step-grandfather came late one night, whilst we were sitting around the fire having a sing song, listening to one of my grandmother's Romany songs: he was very drunk and looking for trouble. We were quiet, fearful of giving him a reason to become more aggressive. He started to pick on Mary's husband, Jack, a sailor who was home on leave prior to being

73

discharged. He had a bad time in the war, spending time adrift on an open boat after his ship was sunk by a submarine. Jack was sitting opposite me, telling him to behave himself and go away or go to bed. He did eventually go - cursing as he staggered away. Jack lifted his hands for us to see how they were shaking in temper. He said the old fool had come very close to getting hit by him.

My grandfather had fought in the First World War for the British but, because he came from Southern Ireland, he had to be domiciled there for a number of years before returning to England. He had a broken nose, cauliflower ears, and scars over his eyebrows. He had been a bare-knuckle pugilist in the past and boxed at Plumstead Baths on Saturdays for twenty-five shillings a night, taking on all comers. This way of life, I assumed, caused him to become psychotic when drunk: eager to fight anyone. In the area of Slades Green and Erith he was known as *'Bayonet Collins'*. To his close family he was nicknamed *'Marra'*, or Harry. How he came by these names other than Harry I do not know, but if you knew about him anything would have suited.

The war with Germany was now over, but we were still at war with Japan. A rumour quickly spread that the war with Japan had also ceased and everyone began to dance and sing hysterically, shouting the good news to each other, glad that we were free to live in peace at last. The following day was one of despondency, when the truth dawned that we had all been fooled. It was easy for this to happen: we didn't have portable radios then or wireless. But we all felt better for it when it happened, having such a good time bucked us up for a while, imagining peace had come at last. This tendency to exaggerate was again displayed when it was rumoured that a German plane had been shot down near the camp some months previously. It was said that the pilot's private parts were seen hanging from a branch of a nearby tree. This tale was told to me by more than one person, all swearing it to have been true. I suppose, once again, it shows how foolishly rumours were believed without having contact with the outside world.

My first sexual experience occurred by chance with the sister of the older boy who'd used me to achieve sexual fulfilment in the toilet of our house. He only lived a short distance along the road and one morning, after a raid, I went to their shelter about something or other. His sister was also there. He asked me to come down after I called from the entrance. Taking off my shoes, I squeezed into bed with them both. He went to the house, whereupon I snuggled closer to his sister, who was very pretty with long brown hair. I began to ask about her boyfriend and what he did when they were together. Things like, *"does he do this?"* as I began to kiss her, then asked her other things that he did as I lay on top of her. I now had an erection and I was beginning to probe her, asking if he did this or that, as I searched for the entrance to her body. She began to help me by saying *"a little to the left"*, then the right, until I found the right place. With the joy the feeling gave as I entered her body saying *"bull's-eye"* I began the rhythm of sexual union for the first time. I soon reached a climax with this warm adorable beauty, only to hear her father's voice asking, *"Whose shoes are these laying by the door?"*

She quickly replied that they were mine and that I had let her brother have them to try on, as I was selling them. My heart was thumping so loud, as I cowered in the corner trying to make myself as small as possible. Her father made his way to the house, tired after working all night and not in the mood to take any other action. She moved out towards the exit saying for me to get out after a few minutes. I quickly leapt the garden fences as I went, wearing the offending shoes and carrying the agony and ecstasy of that early morning awakening.

I never had the good fortune to repeat it with her, but saw her on one occasion by the American Army Camp at Old Bexley waiting for a soldier friend. Another time, in the bedroom of their house, the brother snatched off her knickers, placed his hands either side of her exposed vagina, opening it wider for me to see and said: *"Look at that, Ron - what a lovely c... that is"*. I felt sorry for her, being treated in such a way, assuming he must have been intimate with her sexually to behave as he did. Being with her in the shelter during the raids would no doubt have aroused him with his level of libido, sister or not. After all, he used me on two occasions to satisfy his craving for sex. I'm sure he would have been tempted to abuse his sister when the chance came. I felt sad and robbed of the tenderness and joy of discovery I had shared with her because of his debasing action.

Leaving School

I left school at Christmas 1945, before my fourteenth birthday (a concession on the part of the head, as I was one or two days past the leaving date that would have meant my having to do another three months until the Easter term). I thanked him when he explained the difference in the dates and was glad to be leaving at last. The big day came, when the whole school assembled in the hall to see the leavers have their hands shaken by the head, with good luck wishes for the future.

When it came to my turn he said, *"Well done Farquhar; you've done very well over the last eighteen months and would have gone into the A stream had you stayed longer. Come round to my office before you go, I want to see you."* He called me in, then, going to the desk drawer, brought out the lighter and cigarettes saying, *"I thought you would like one of these now"* and bade me farewell as he placed the offending booty in my outstretched hand - instilling in me forever a respect for authority figures who are genuine and fair. Later in my life I was to meet quite a few who didn't fit this category.

I went to a dance arranged by the Army Cadets and, whilst waiting by the entrance to the 'Hall' on a warm evening among a small jostling crowd, saw the same young blonde girl whom I had kissed as she walked along the narrow path with her friend. She was wearing a grey crepe tight-fitting dress which invited my arm to encircle her slim body. Feeling pleasure from the touch of the dress fabric coupled with the contour of her slender hips sent me into a sensual rapture that seemed to ignite the blood coursing my body, firing it with desire for her. I couldn't speak, nor understand what was happening to me, or the rapture I experienced. I never saw her again but wondered if she felt the same as I? I was now smitten with strong feelings for many girls whom I was loosely acquainted with, either to know or just those that I may see on occasion without speaking to. I would think of these girls with great longing. Unable to make any contact with them, I had this agonising longing of unrequited puppy love.

One such girl was Sheila Greer who lived in Slades Green and would be found playing outside her house most evenings in the summer of my fourteenth year. Another older fellow had an interest in her – his attempt to make an impression on her involved throwing me to the ground and looking at her for some recognition of his strength. She had long, naturally blonde hair with a stunning face to match. Another who took much of my time, dreaming of her quiet manner and beauty, and the most attractive of all, was Lena Lee, a gypsy.

I first knew Lena when I was thirteen. She was my age and just as tall, with raven black hair that hung halfway down her back. I couldn't take my eyes off her whenever she was around. She was joy itself to behold.

Trips to my grandmother's, which culminated in being with her, were well worth the effort. Unfortunately she died, suddenly breaking her neck when some fools had lifted a five-barred gate from its hinges, leaving it propped against the post. When Lena, full of life, ran to swing on the gate, she broke her neck as it hit the ground. What a tragic end to such a wonderful girl, through the stupidity of a mindless act.

By now my father had been discharged from the army, after agreeing to make a new start with my mother. This made me happier than I had ever been since the start of the war. My father bought me a bike from a fellow that worked in the docks, who also found him a job there. I was now working at 'Bert Bolton and Haywood's, as a Saw Doctor's Apprentice. My life was now complete, with us all together and my father uniting the family.

It was arranged for me to go away with the army cadets to Folkestone, but before going I told my father about letters my mother was getting from her old flame, Lofty in Woolwich Barracks. When I returned home, as I was going through the front door, I saw my mother's face was a mass of bruises - both eyes blackened, a swollen nose and discoloured. She said, *"Look what your father has done to me."* I brushed past her, thinking, *"you deserved it".* My whole world then collapsed as before, leaving a great hole. Where, for a short time, there had been love, I was left another blank hollow once again full of hatred.

I blamed her again for the trouble she'd caused, breaking up the family, making us all unhappy by her deceit - when everything had at last seemed perfect in our lives.

I left the Army cadets, telling many lies at the Employment Office to leave my job in the factory. In those days, just after the war, there was a law that prevented anyone leaving employment if it came under what was known as 'The Essential Works Order' *(that meant anyone employed in work contributing to the regeneration of the country was not allowed to leave).* As the company manufactured scaffold boards, I had to have a very good reason to leave. I did feel guilty when the fellows asked me to send them some Devonshire cream (before leaving I had lied, saying I was going to the Dartmouth Naval Academy to join the navy). The following week I was working as a labourer on a building site.

My brother Bob had been arrested for stealing a bicycle from a neighbour. He saw it lying on the ground, so borrowed it for a ride, knowing who owned it. The boy reported it missing and the police were called, charging my brother when he returned it to the owner. He was given a caution, but it still counted as an offence and the beginning of a long record.

Taking the Other Road

Keep to the right road Ronnie; don't be like your
Bertrums
And take the crooked one:

* * * * *

And the child said to me in a dream
Habitual strength is no stronger than
Habitual weakness,
The habitual hero is no hero,
The habitual weakling has found his
Marvellous level
Who knows, for another good from evil?
The only strong are as the Angel, who is half devil.
Conrad Aiken

The last line expressed my make up at the time, aged fourteen.

During my fourteenth year, after the break-up of the marriage and my father leaving, I read an article in Readers' Digest about Eddie Chapman, the British double agent. Eddie Chapman had been a safe blower before the war and was captured by the Germans while being detained in the Channel Islands awaiting deportation to England for crimes he'd committed. Reading this was to instil in me an ambition that would affect my life just as assuredly as if I had been programmed from birth.

Becoming a safe blower would answer all my problems: I would help my family rise from the poverty we had experienced, and satisfy all our needs. I didn't think about the moral aspect of it: once again, my paradigm structure as a lad of fourteen was limited having to few options for the position I was in. I was willing to take my chances and not heed the words of my grandmother: *"Keep to the right road Ronnie, don't be like your Bertrums and take the crooked one."* I had taken detonators from incendiary bombs without fearing the consequences, climbed trees others wouldn't and, of course, continued playing cricket when the siren went. Being a safe blower was the all same to me: I just didn't care. Would I have done the same thing had I come from a different background? Taken responsibility and put on a brave face when taking my younger siblings into the shelter during the raids? The influence also of my father's stealing no doubt led me to take the other road. If my mother had been loyal to my father I wouldn't have taken the road to crime. I would have been daring, ambitious, perhaps even foolhardy - but not a criminal.

The decision to become a safe blower affected me in a most profound way, because I then sublimated my sexual drive to achieve my goal. Of course I was completely unaware of this, but reasoned I didn't want to get emotionally involved with women because they would have to wait for me if I went to prison. I didn't want to be responsible for that happening to another person. That was how I saw my future: without any commitment other than to crime. I did not want to have children under those circumstances, conscious of the problems it would cause.

I had my first drink in my fifteenth year, with my future partner in crime who lived in our road. The fellow had a cruel streak, always being the first to offer some weird punishment or initiation task to anyone wanting to be part of the gang. One of his ploys was for the initiate to go down a manhole and have the cover placed on top while others would sit on it, making it impossible to get out. Being tied to a tree and having a saucepan placed on your head, until such time as they saw fit to release you, was another of his favoured tests.

He hadn't changed. Getting a kick out of seeing how stupidly I'd behave with my first drink was part of his cruelty. We palled up together a year later, making a good team and lucky with it. I liked the taste of beer and became friendly with John, the son of the painted doll. We would go to Dartford on pub crawls, to get drunk and act the goat. Once we climbed up the front of the Town Hall at Crayford to get into the dance.

During these trips to Dartford we would meet some of the local middle-aged homosexuals on the train. They would try to engage us in conversation, telling us of their exploits such as how the local villains would suspect them of being coppers and then leave the pubs they went into. Occasionally they would mention parties they were having and invite us, but we were wise to their tricks. They were always in good humour though, unconcerned about their homosexuality: although in those days of course it was taboo and a criminal offence. My drinking partner eventually met a middle-class girl called Faun, who had her own horse. I never saw much of him after that. As he'd learnt to ride as an evacuee, I assumed they spent their time together.

One Sunday afternoon, as I was going to the cinema in Erith with my uncle Bert and his girlfriend Franny, Bert saw someone across the road, standing by the bus stop with a young lad. Bert told us to stand in the doorway of a shop and wait for him. He brought the fellow back and they immediately joined in avid conversation, using prison slang terms that were all new to me. After a while the fellow turned to Bert, asking if I was all right to be trusted as he continued the conversation. Bert told Franny he would see her later, and left us together. He then told me what had happened in language I could understand.

It transpired that the man had known Bert in Chelmsford nick: they had been on the same wing. The fellow had escaped two nights previously and was standing with the boy in the hope of diverting suspicion from him if the police had checked him out. So it was arranged for him to stay with us. I would introduce him as a fellow in the merchant navy, a friend of Bert willing to pay for his keep. I knew my mother wouldn't turn her nose up at any money she could make. We took him home and all was well with my mother, as I guessed it would be. He was keen to get money, asking Bert the best places to break into. I listened to him enthralled, particularly by his account of how he got out of prison; by the way he got into a farmhouse the first night, waking the woman in the house but keeping his cool when she asked, *"Who's there?"* and replying, *"don't worry its only me"* as he went about stealing money, clothing and food. How he escaped was itself an act that thrilled me in the telling. I was impressed by the exploits of this man who came into my life for me to learn from.

On the second night, he broke into a house where Bert said money could be found. Our friend was annoyed, finding a man with a wage packet that had only fifteen pounds in it. *"I couldn't take a bloke's wages"* he said, *"so I left it"*.

He was called the Dragon Man: he had a dragon tattooed on each arm. The evening papers said the search for the 'Dragon Man' had widened and the net was closing in on him, as there had been sightings. His real name was Joseph Purton. At one time he had been a plumber and carried a plumber's knife, which he said was the best tool to use when breaking in anywhere. I believe he had also served in the army. One morning, after he had been at our house for about a week, Joe came into my room and said, *"Here kid, come and hold this bag will you?"* I did as he asked, picking up an old weather-beaten Gladstone type bag, like those used by doctors. Joe said, *"Open it"*. It contained more money than I had ever seen in my life. Joe continued, *"You will never have as much in your hands as that, kid, there's two and a half thousand pounds there. Here kid, take this and hide it"* throwing me a five-pound bag of silver. Bert then came in, asked me the best place to buy a car and for directions to get there.

They gave me money for the fares, but Bert told me off after we got off the bus because I hadn't bought 'Workman's Returns'. That was the first and only bus Bert had ever been on so early in the morning, never having worked in his life. They both bought cars: Joe a red sports model and Bert a Jaguar that he was forever cleaning.

Remand and Sentence

I was charged with some other fellows for burgling a bungalow and sent to Maidstone Quarter Sessions for sentence. I was remanded in custody at Harrietsham near Maidstone. As soon as I arrived, the head of staff - a man called Conlin - had it in for me because of my surly attitude, demonstrated by my not calling him 'Sir'. I was placed under what I have since learnt was called *'Pin Down'*, which required me to be segregated from the others at night for two weeks. I found the time in the attic room quite peaceful, with the cooing sound of turtle doves to serenade me each night an added joy.

When joining the rest of the fellows, I was pleased to find that my friend and drinking partner John, the son of the Painted Doll, had now joined our merry band. I cannot recall the reason for his being there, nor what happened to him when he was sentenced, but I was destined to meet up with him later in life.

As friends, we were allowed to work together during the day. We were fortunate to have a decent fellow supervising us both. The other inmates were not so lucky, having a mixed-race man of Indian descent who worked them hard, using the words "*Tushka Tushka*" the whole day long and not letting them stop for a break until the official time. It was hard working in the sun, and being half starved if you didn't have food parcels sent in by your family. Our officer - named Frost - had a good heart, and whenever we were in the garden tool-shed together he would split a cigarette in half for us to share. He did this often when away from the main building. Once there was a delivery of coke that we had to shovel away from the dropping area in the cellar. For this, he gave us ten cigarettes, as we got so bloody dirty with all the dust flying about. It is people like him that smooth the hard knocks you experience in Institutions, God bless them.

We had to march everywhere in alphabetical order, so I was with a chap called Fougher: we were also on the same table for meals. Lunch usually consisted of six slices of bread, a pat of butter the size of a chequers counter, and an orange. Needless to say, we were so hungry that we put the peel between the slices to make sandwiches. I watched tears fall down Fougher's face one day when he said he was starving hungry. The day came when Conlin stood up, declaring that a kindly local farmer had offered the cook some strawberries that we could have with the evening meal followed by cream! Most of us just gazed in amazement, until the slow process of eating began. I cut each of mine four times: I had thirty-two of the blighters and I'm sure Fougher and the others knew how many they had.

Whilst I was there I met a fellow from Chatham called Poole. His brother was killed by a police marksman when peering from a bedroom window. He was suspected of having a shotgun. The family was well known by the local police and was hounded by them during the war years. The brother who was killed had made a place to hide in his back garden, to avoid the constant searches by the police. It was the first account I recall of the police shooting someone. I think they over-reacted and should never have killed the fellow.

The day came for me to go to court and I was sent to reside in a Hostel at Forest Gate, London for six months. I was now fifteen and six months. My mother came to the court and gave me ten cigarettes and some cherries. I was driven to London by a female probation officer and a male companion who chatted together all the way, ignoring me the whole time as if I were some inanimate parcel. The woman dropped us off at an underground station. My escort then asked me a few questions, finishing by saying, *"It seems to me you have had too many bites of the cherry laddy"*. I wondered how he knew that, for I had been surreptitiously eating the cherries my mother had given me, dumping the stones on the floor of the car. Feeling guilty at being found out, I replied, *"Yes, sir"*. I'd never heard the expression before!

The Hostel at Earlham Grove, Forest Gate was a violent place. I was fifteen, tall and skinny. I went through the induction, *"Welcome, behave yourself, and you will be all right"* routine from the Super. He was a short, portly, retired sea captain, whose wife acted as matron: they were both in their sixties. I was first approached by a lad named Williams, who asked whether I had any fags. I duly gave him one as he told me, *"Oatway's the 'daddy' and I am number two. Oatway hasn't got long to do. Most of the fellows here work in the silk factory in Stratford - Angel Lane - that's where you will go no doubt. Give us another fag for later will you?"* I once again obliged. Then I was accosted by Sturtevant, a short thin chap with blonde hair, who also tapped me for a fag before taking me to a cupboard, pulling out a cut-throat razor that he'd hidden, and saying, *"Anyone messes with me will get this. My old man's a bookie at Walthamstow Dogs and Sturtevant ain't my real name: it's Harris. But those bastards don't know that, OK! See you later".* With that he was gone; leaving me to unravel what had just taken place with just two of England's so-called juvenile delinquents. I was one of the youngest in the place, which held around sixteen (eight in each dormitory). The eldest - eighteen or over - were waiting to go for National Service.

I started work for a local building firm called Howlets: a shop fitter on the Romford Road. I was a plumber's mate working with a fellow recently discharged from the Navy, the son of the foreman. He was in his early twenties and easy to get along with. I enjoyed the time I spent with the firm and in particular with Charlie the plumber who taught me quite a lot of the trade while I was there.

When we were working we were allowed to keep some of the money for ourselves, and the rest went on our keep. There was one large room where we gathered at night: we were not allowed out at all. The only amusement was a small billiard table and three bent cues. To relieve the monotony we would play 'truth or dare', going round the group in turn. On one occasion I was to take the billiard balls and cues back into the 'Super' and say, *"Here's the fucking balls super, stick them up your fucking arse, we are all fucking fed up with them."* I did this, shouting the first five or six words so the listeners at the door could hear, but then I closed the door to the Super's office and rattled off the last words as I opened it on the way out and was duly acknowledged as having passed the dare.

One of the most cruel and vicious tricks was to get a new fellow to play 'catch the diver'. It would happen to the dupe a few days after he arrived, when he was still somewhat disorientated and willing to play along with whatever was asked of him, hoping to ingratiate himself with the lads. The trick was to get the fellow to hold the hands of one of the tougher guys and to catch the diver, as he jumped from a top window into their arms. The dupe would then hold tight to the hands of the other catcher, only to get his face smashed in by the head of the other catcher as the diver fell into their arms. The screams of the unsuspecting dupe would ring out, as blood from his (perhaps) broken nose poured out over the floor. There would be profuse apologies, from both the diver and the other catcher, saying it was an accident and hadn't happened before, which added greatly to the enjoyment of the onlookers, laughing profusely at the plight of the fellow who by now had gone in to see Matron to get repaired. Nothing ever came of these escapades, as I believe it was somewhat expected and seen simply as letting off steam: there weren't any other ways of expressing our energy, such as football or games of any kind.

One day, a fellow complained about a large boil he had on the side of his head, between his ear and cheekbone. He said that it hurt and would like it out. One fellow quipped, *"I know a way I saw it done to a pal of mine: it worked by putting a milk bottle half-filled with steam on it."* A half-filled bottle came from somewhere and was immediately plonked on the casualty's offending boil, which began to disappear into the steamed bottle accompanied by the screams of the fellow, whose eye was now nearing the bottle's entrance as it was being sucked in, as explained by the knowledgeable informant. I believe the bottle was smashed just in time but cannot remember ever seeing the fellow again.

Another time one of the wags thought it a good wheeze to steal an eel from a fish shop and put it in the bed of a fellow delinquent. All went well until the fellow looked at what was making him cold in the feet area, and then all hell broke loose. The police were called to apprehend the offending snake-like object and charge the thief, who was banished to one of His Majesty's Reformatory Schools, until he had learned to behave in a 'civilised manner,' like fellow wheeze types at Eton and Harrow. They would get away with far worse japes as part of their Rag week, and nothing would be said about the stolen eel, as daddy would send a cheque for a tenner. There was one thing in favour of the prankster: his little escapade made the national press, thus giving him some sort of kudos wherever he went.

I had my first run-in with Davis, a tough fellow from Swansea, two years my senior and twice as powerful muscle wise. He took from me a paper I was reading and refused to give it back. *'I borrowed it,'* he said and insisted that I had lost it. When I snatched it back from him, he offered me to go out to the toilets and fight. I may have hit him once or twice, but I was no match in age and strength for this streetwise tearaway from the valleys. I was hit for the first time by another's head and bashed against the door, punched about the face until I said I had had enough. I then went to clean my face up in the nearby sink. Still seething at the liberty of taking my paper, I didn't give in to his threats of another beating and I was still arguing with him as I cleaned my face in the sink.

I was allowed home at weekends if I could produce a letter from my mother, so I would write my own once a fortnight, asking if Ronnie could be allowed home. I was never refused, as I think they were glad to get you out of the way, making one less for them to worry about. One day, at home in Erith reading the *News of the World,* I saw a beautiful girl's picture in the 'missing from home' section. Her name was Yvonne Hanson from Edmonton, London, aged fifteen. *"Why can't I meet someone like her?"* I asked my mother. The next time I came home she was there. Her hair had been dyed black; she was six feet tall, and a stunner. She was with my mother's cousin, Israel, the fellow who had his handcuffs taken off in our loo. He also had his brother, Robert living with him. By now Israel had a profitable haulage business and a yard, where local villains used to have safes opened with his cutting equipment at the generous price of fifty percent of whatever they contained. It was no wonder that Yvonne, the young, intelligent, confused, admiring beauty had become a gangster groupie. I got to know her a little better when we shared journeys back to the hostel: I learned she wrote poetry, liked Hoagy Carmichael the singer, and was besotted with Israel and his contacts.

I had another run-in with Davis when the tea wasn't to his liking and he told everyone not to drink it. I refused, and got another beating in the toilets for my trouble. I waited a couple of weeks, and then nicked his money and sweet coupons from his pockets while he was asleep. He had coupons he'd stolen from other fellows, so I was more than pleased at his outburst the next morning when he cursed everyone, saying he would kill whoever had taken them. I felt avenged, getting one over on him, but it took me many years to completely forget him. I often had thoughts of going to Swansea to get my revenge. After the second beating I was asked by Robinson, a pal of Davis back home in Swansea, if I still fancied my chances with him. I said I did but knew I was just bragging, for what chance did I have with someone of his age and fighting experience? Robinson went on to tell me of Davis's probation officer who had asked him why he kept fighting the lads in Swansea when, if he wanted a good fight, he could go down to see the 'pit boys'. They would oblige him, he said, as they fight with their clogs on and surely that should satisfy him. I often overheard Davis speaking of his local pub, the Gower Arms in Swansea, where he was well known. I didn't forget my need for revenge on him until long after my twentieth birthday.

Robinson had the best job of us all: he worked in a hand-made sweet firm called [Mario Maranta's], located in Cambridge Circus, just near Tottenham Court Road. He would come home at night and say, *"You'd never guess who was in our shop today buying the best chocolates."* We would quip back something stupid like *"Old Mother Riley"* or *"Mickey Mouse"* and he would say, *"James Mason"* or some other famous person. It was all true but we were jealous of him.

Occasionally, a few of us would climb out of the window to go to the West End to see the lights - just to have a break from the place. The last time we did this, my wallet fell from my pocket as I scrambled back through the window: a neighbour heard us and called the police. When they came in we gave them a good reception saying, *"What's the trouble, waking us all up etc."* We had no respect for them and didn't hold back on our cursing. I was told to get out of bed as my wallet was found and was asked for an explanation. I lied, saying it was just me: no-one else had been out. Nothing came of it anyway. When they gave me back my diary, the Super drew attention to some doggerel I'd written in it. *"Now I'm at the end of this verse.... If they lock me up it will make me worse"*. I was alluding to my defiance of the justice system and prison, at age fifteen.

Nearing the end of my sentence, I had a visit from the probation officer, a Mr Coles from Dartford, to arrange for my visits to him after the release date.

My mother, during my time away, was still going with different men, although the war was over. Israel had gone back to Edmonton, but not before he had made a mess of the face of the bloke my mother was sleeping with. This fellow, I assume, made a pass at Yvonne and Israel had taken the top layer of skin from his face with a leather strap that had small shoe brads protruding from it. Scraped around your face a few times, this is enough to '*let you know you have been a*

97

naughty boy' to use the parlance of the time. He later received ten years' imprisonment for cutting off a man's hand with a bayonet.

The local head of police shot himself for being involved with Israel, having taken bribes for favours. Israel and his gang were responsible for blowing a strong room in Hertford Town Hall, stealing the clothing coupons for the whole of Hertfordshire - necessitating their reprinting. During the war, clothing coupons could be exchanged on the black market for as much as a half-crown each, which meant they were worth a lot of money. There were still many restrictions in force, even though the war had ended, such as saving electricity by not having street lights on at night, and allowing factories to work 24 hours a day to get the country back on its feet.

One night my mother came home with the fellow that Israel had attacked with the knuckleduster, and started to have sex with him, making such a noise I couldn't sleep. I thought of my sister and aunt in the other room having to put up with it as well. I had once seen a film about gangsters, where one puts a belt around his fist to beat his opponent. I had heard enough and, wrapping the belt round my fist, went into the bedroom, first making a noise fumbling when undoing the door which was enough to make the man disappear from the bed to hide under it. My mother was still on the bed naked: I was shocked, seeing her dark brown skin, as I shouted for them to pack it in. I had had enough listening to them, adding some more curses about what I would do. There was another couple sleeping in the front room downstairs, wanting to know what all the noise was for. My mother had come down the stairs by now and began to argue with me saying 'why can't she have a man, and what's wrong with it?' It got heated and she went for me: in self-defence I struck her with my fist to stop her. Then I left to go to my grandmother's. I told her what had happened and she said, *"You're too old now to put up with all her carryings on"*. I slept with all my aunts and gran that night in one large bed: all five of us. The next day I went back home and nothing was said, but my mother never did it again while I was there.

I came home from the hostel to find just my sister there: my two brothers had been before the courts again and been sent away for their own 'care and protection' to a National Children's Home. I then teamed up with the fellow in the road who bought me my first drink, going out at night under cover of the dark nights, breaking into shops and pubs. We would meet at his house, making sure the lights were out while we made special covers to go over our torches - the small penlight type. We made sure we wore gloves for this exercise, in case we left our fingerprints on the cigarette packets we used to make the narrow funnels that covered the lighted end. We knew all the back alleys to get from A to B, without using roads where we might be seen by police patrols. We broke into the A & C club at Erith, getting into the kitchen area easily but being stopped by the locked door leading to the bar. Noticing that the stone step was worn and the key was still in the lock on the opposite side, we put some newspaper under the door as we dislodged the key with a forks prong, allowing it to fall on the paper, then pulling it from under the door to let ourselves into the bar. We found little in the way of money or cigarettes, so left more or less empty handed, though glad to have achieved the purpose of getting into the place without waking the tenants in the rooms above. We did think about going up the stairs, but they creaked too much and there was also a bright light left on at the top. It was easy getting around with soft, crepe-soled shoes, wearing black or dark clothes, going through side roads, alleys and making good use of parks and allotments.

Soon my friend went off to do his National Service so I palled up with another fellow from school, doing much the same thing - breaking into pubs and houses at night. We got into one on a foggy night after the ban on street lighting was lifted and watched a couple of police having a chat at the telephone box, less than a hundred yards away. We found money there, but only copper coins in large ten-pound bags so we only took one. We did more break-ins over the course of the following year. I spoke to my Probation Officer about finding me a place to live, as I wasn't getting along with my step-dad Joe who was now living with my mother. It was only partly true, but my main reason was to get away from Erith before the police caught up with me.

I made it a rule never to mix socially, say in cafes, the cinema or pubs, with the person I was stealing with. Eventually, the fellow with me did something by himself and spoke about it in a local café. He was soon arrested, making the national papers as a young sixteen year-old responsible for over a hundred burglaries in the Kent area. This, of course, was not true, but the Kent police had a way of saying to offenders, *"look, if you take these other jobs into consideration we will do what we can to help you"*. It was a lie, of course, but it did get the books cleared, so to speak, and help in their promotion.

The fellow went to the '*Akbar'*, a notorious Naval Training Ship. Berthed in Liverpool, it was run by bullies whose sole task was to break the spirit of those in their charge. My friend never forgot his time there: like the many others who had the misfortune to go there, he was mentally scarred for the rest of his life.

I was still stealing from various places in and around Erith, Welling, and Bexleyheath, mainly from houses at night when the occupants were asleep. Then my Probation Officer took me to Chiswick - St Christopher's Hostel at 13 Bolton Road. After the second night I broke into the Railway Hotel by climbing in through an open window on the first floor. It led into a bedroom where an older woman was sleeping. I went through this bedroom and down some stairs where there were more doors, but they were all locked. I went back out through the same window without taking anything, for fear of waking the woman. I then made my way to another house that had some makeshift repair to the casement window, entering by squeezing my hand through the gap by removing the repair. I undid the larger window and made my entrance into a living room that contained an erect ironing board, children's clothing strewn in disarray about the room, and some clean napkins. I found a small amount of money to tide me over and then went back to the hostel, content at my first night's exploration of the area and my first experience of being on my own in the bedroom of a sleeping person.

The hostel contained young men who, in the main, were from homes without parents, as well as others, such as me, who couldn't get on with them for various reasons. The fellow running it was called Hardachre. We had to call him *'brother'* and even louder when he'd put his hand in your pocket to grab your dick or balls until you screamed to make him stop. I worked for a local building firm called 'Knapps', assisting in the repair of bomb-damaged houses within four miles of their depot. Brother Hardachre often asked me what I did when I went out by myself, as I didn't mix much with the others unless told to.

Once we had to go to another hostel at Twickenham for a boxing match. I did well in the first two rounds but, having no skills at all, was well and truly beaten in the last by someone who knew his boxing. On another occasion we were given tickets to see the 'Canadian All Stars' play an English team at Ice Hockey. It was a first for me and I enjoyed it.

On the way home, I saved a chap's life at Chiswick Park Station because of my quick thinking. It was raining hard as we walked from the train toward the exit. Suddenly a fellow running up the stairs jumped into the nearly closing doors. In the gloomy light I saw what appeared to be a sack blow under the train, but I could not be sure whether or not it was a person. So, running to the train and placing my arm down into the gap between the train and platform, I began to wave at the guard as he looked out at me, ready to signal for the train to start on its journey. He shouted, *"What's up?"* and I shouted back, *"A man on the line"*. As he left the guard's van and came over to me I told him, *"I'm sure someone has fallen under the train two carriages up"*. He went for his light, then to where I had seen the incident take place, and we found a man entwined amongst the tubes and cables. The guard spoke to the driver to have the current turned off: I then bent down and grabbed him by the arms, moving him enough to allow others to help me pull him out. He was a dead weight, having no doubt fainted at the fear of his imminent death.

What was so surreal about the whole episode was that people in the carriages just sat reading their papers, oblivious to what was occurring outside their carriages, even though this struggle between life and death was occurring just a few feet from them. While he was being removed from the cables and placed on the platform, a voice within me said, *"You will be rewarded, get away from here"*. So I went back to the hostel with my companion, who was struck dumb by the incident and unable to help in any way. Thanks to my quick thinking, weighing up the situation as I had, I managed to save the life of a drunken Irishman who happened to trip up when running for a train in the pouring rain. I could smell his breath as we took him up from the line and had only to see his face to know he was Irish. A few days later, Brother came to congratulate me for my action, saying I was a hero: my companion had told others what I had done.

My father found employment as a Commissionaire at the Chicken Inn in the Haymarket. He had to wear a uniform and loved the job - flirting with the waitresses, getting cabs for the customers and receiving tips that helped keep him in ready money. He got nylon stockings from the many Yanks still around in London at the time, and sold them to the waitresses.

Meanwhile, my friend from Erith had served his two years' National Service in the army and was eager to get back to our old way of life, doing various crimes in and around the district. I spent time with them both, drinking in the West End and still not interested in women. I enjoyed the shows that were to be seen at the Chiswick Empire and, of course, films as well.

This time I could afford to see the best in the West End, as well as shows at the Palladium where I saw Hoagy Carmichael top the bill. He played the piano with an orange, asking the audience to give him a couple of notes then using them to create a song.

I was now returning frequently to Erith, teaming up with R who had done his army time. His home life was not so good: his mother was seeing another man, who would regularly walk up and down the road, looking into their front room to see her. R's father was a small man, who did nothing to stop the arrangement. R never mentioned living under those circumstances, but it must have affected his life. We both had something in common on that score. One of our best robberies happened by chance when we broke into a local pub. We fed pub crisps to the dog, a little Scottie, while we emptied the tills, which held quite a bit of money. R told me there had been a celebration - for the Christening or birth of the Prince of Wales. The governor hadn't bothered to empty the tills, as he was too tired. It was a very cold night and the front of my sports jacket was frozen stiff. We went to R's house to split the money. I went back to the hostel cock a hoop at my good fortune, better off by £40 - a month's work or more for a man in those days.

When going to meet my father and R soon after the pub episode I was approached on the train by a young American Air Force chap in civvies, who asked me what racket I was in. Bragging, I said, "*Nylons from*

American PX s." He quipped back, saying he could get me some good deals in cigarettes - very cheap. He then opened the top pocket of his black leather jacket and showed me a large wad of notes in a tightly bulging pocket. I was impressed at seeing such an amount and duly parted with a fiver, thinking of all the cigarettes I would sell, making a good profit. He gave me an address in New York to write to, where his mother would send them on to me. My father laughed his head off, saying I'd been conned and would never see any cigarettes. The fellow was no doubt travelling on the train all day, catching mugs like me. I was to be tricked again, this time by a team of crooks at the races, which showed my naivety outside the limited structures of my experience.

No growth in the areas of relationships, feminine company, or social mores. I had chosen this narrow myopic path, blind to the difficulties that lay outside it - once again feeling deeply alienated. However, I later experienced more situations like this as I struggled to live a normal life away from crime. Brother would call me aside on the odd occasion, asking where I went when I was not at the hostel. I couldn't say home, for he knew I had left because of problems there. I decided to say *"with my father"* and this seemed to go down well enough with him. One day, while sprinting up the stone steps of the hostel entrance, I fell hard on my chin. I went to Hammersmith Hospital where a young girl stitched me up, laying my head on her soft breasts. I realised what

I had been missing as I enjoyed the closeness of her body. But that was all.

On another trip to the hunting area of Erith, we broke into a shop a hundred yards from the Police Station, stealing women's dresses that we carried over our arms as we made our way back to R's house by the most devious of ways. We barely crossed a road to get there. It was the Sunday that clothing coupons ceased to be necessary for buying clothes. I came back the next week to collect my cut from the sale of the stuff, which had been done by a friend of R's in Woolwich.

It was about this time that I met up with my first serious drinking partner from Erith, the son of painted doll who was with me in the Remand Home. I was walking through the Underground concourse at Piccadilly, near a well known haunt for gays, and looked hard at a fellow dressed in a camel coloured coat and wearing dark glasses. I peered under them, recognising my old pal, and I spoke his name. He said, *"Hello Ron"* in a slow drawl without any emotion at all. I asked him if he was waiting for anyone and he replied, *"Whoever comes"* in the same dead soulless voice. I arranged to meet him later and on two occasions he explained he'd become a male prostitute after associating with the middle-aged Erith gays who took him to one of their parties where it all began. I saw him some years later, picking up cigarette butts in the gutter along Oxford Street dressed as a tramp. He looked round at me, rubbing his chin the way he always did when thinking about something. I soon lost sight of him in the crowd.

I cannot remember how I came to lose contact with R. It could have been when he stole a suit from the same shop we had burgled and was caught wearing it in the town. He gave some story about buying it from someone in a pub and was given three months' imprisonment for receiving. I met up with my uncle Bert and we went to Gravesend drinking. We walked around most of the night trying to steal a car to get us back to Erith. We eventually found one with keys in, after looking in the garages of private houses. We manoeuvred the thing from the garage and drove it home, not realising it was nearly out of petrol. So we broke into a roadside garage to get a fill up. It was a very hot sunny morning by now and while we were trying to find out how the pumps worked a fellow pulled up and asked if we could sell him some petrol. We said we were closed and he drove away. We moved off without getting any, deciding to go as far as we could. Further along the road, a police car swerved in front of us. We ran over the hill to our right, with the police following along the narrow lanes around Gravesend. Bert got away but I was caught running towards Gravesend Station by a uniformed copper. As soon as he held me I thought *'Borstal, here I come.'*

I was put on remand in Canterbury Prison, a Young Offender charged with breaking into the garage and stealing the car. I was sentenced at Maidstone Quarter

Sessions by the worst judge presiding, called Thesinger, who frequently commented on how hard he would come down on the criminals from London who came down to steal from the law-abiding residents of Kent. I saw tough fellows come down to the cells, crying over the severity of the sentences they were given, for they were getting from five to seven years, with little chance of remission, for the most petty of crimes. This was because of the new Labour government under Attlee, who introduced what was known as 'Preventive Detention' and 'Corrective Training'. If you were under thirty, and had appeared before an Assize or Quarter Sessions on two occasions, you were given Corrective Training, which meant you were to learn a trade. If you had appeared three times you were given 'Preventive Detention', which meant you only got one seventh of your sentence off in remission. It was a farce, and a most punitive law, because it meant that you could be put away for a long time for stealing a bottle of milk from a doorstep or a pair of socks from Woolworth's. I knew a man, Pat O'Connor, who was a petty crook and an alcoholic. Once, in a pub, a friend gave him some articles which had been stolen from a house nearby. When he was taken to the police station for being drunk and disorderly, the articles were found on his person and he was charged with committing the burglary and sentenced to seven years' imprisonment for a crime he didn't commit. He went on many hunger strikes while doing his time, suffering dearly for his efforts - so much so that he lost both his appetite and taste for food, on account of the forced feeding he had to undergo. One day, a visitor to the prison told him about Alcoholics Anonymous and it turned his life around. On release, Pat worked hard for the AA organisation, speaking internationally on their behalf for a number of years.

The police caught up with Bert and charged him for being with me when stealing the car. I said my piece in the court, as I had made a statement, but after a lot of wrangling Bert was found guilty. He was at home in the nick at Canterbury, having been there a few times before. He was always in good humour and got on well with the screws, whereas I was given rough treatment because, as a 'Young Offender', I had to be made an example of as it was my first time in prison. I was immediately told off for not calling the doctor 'Sir'.

From there I was sent to Latchmere House Reception Centre near Richmond in Surrey: the intake for the whole of the British Isles. There were fourteen Borstals at that time, with four thousand inmates. They were classified as 'open' or 'enclosed' and you were sent to whichever type of regime was considered appropriate to your circumstances. We had to fill in a form with thirty questions, covering things like 'what is your favourite drink', 'how do you spend your spare time' etc. I didn't want to appear a hard case so I filled in the form accordingly. The woman who took this experiment in psychological assessment was named Gill or Hill.

Through some quirk in my nature, I enjoyed being there amongst my peers. I was now seventeen and a half, still with the ambition of becoming a safe-blower and planning to opt for the 'Sappers' when called for National Service, just so I could learn about explosives. So I was perhaps glad, seeing my plans coming to fruition as I approached ever nearer to achieving my ambition. My mother and Joe visited me, which was good: as did my father on a couple of occasions. Once they all came on the same Saturday and I had to choose who to see. I chose my mother and Joe because they had travelled further.

Latchmere House had housed German officers during the war, and some of their artwork was still to be seen around the place, mainly chalk pastel portraits of attractive blonde women - no doubt lovers left in the Fatherland. We could have cigarettes there but had no means of lighting them when in our cells, so our way of getting cigarettes to light up was to connect the graphite of a pencil to a live wire, wait for it to glow red, then light the end of the fag.

During an evening association period I palled up with a fellow from Catford called Holloway. We would sit for the whole period making up jokes about Jack Benny, the American comedian and his side-kick Rochester, his black stooge who would get the wrong end of the deals Benny set up. It would be in the main about Jack's meanness toward Rochester and we would invent different scenarios where Benny would wriggle out of paying in some way. They went something like this: - Benny and Rochester are in Egypt working as archaeologists; Rochester is doing all the digging and handing out the curios to Benny who is stacking them neatly at the top of the hole. Rochester says that it's all he can do; there aren't any more artefacts left and they will both make plenty of money when they are sold. Benny then begins to fill the excavation from the soil at the top. Rochester is last heard frantically calling out for help, whilst being buried alive so that Benny can save the money he owes him. Such would be the schoolboy humour that we revelled in, each of us inspired by the other's example. We would laugh all night at our ridiculous stories, writhing in pain as we clutched our aching stomachs with joy.

During meal times we were allowed to talk, and a fellow who had spent his life in institutions was eager for me to recount the story of the redcurrant field, where my two friends had taken turns to act out copulation with the young girl. I could only assume that he had never had the company of the opposite sex. Why does no one realise that sexual deviation results from social alienation. This is still happening today because we prevent conjugal visits for prisoners and segregate the sexes when people are incarcerated for long periods. There are many low-grade mental risk prisoners serving time in our institutions, male and female, who would benefit from things like monthly dances or meetings on a social level.

There was a boxing night arranged and I asked this fellow if he would like to box me. I said it without any malice on my part but as he was my height I thought it would be a good match. Once again I came out all blows and no skill and was knocked down three times in the last round. After it was all over, the officer in charge said in his homily that if we showed as much determination in life as we did in the ring tonight we would have no trouble making a success of life on the outside. I felt he was speaking directly to me, since I had got up for more when most would have said 'sod it' and stayed down. My opponent told me the next day that he had been 'All England's Approved Schools Champion' for his weight. I believe my retort was *"Thanks for telling me now"*. I meant it in a jocular manner.

As I was waiting to be allocated a suitable Borstal placing, I worked in the stores with a fellow from Northern Ireland. The officer responsible for our supervision was a Mr Wigley, an ex-copper and a decent fellow in many ways, who showed us kindness throughout the time we were with him. He did us a favour each week, bringing us a tin of dog-ends that his daughter had collected from a dance hall. Being a group leader, I had the extra privilege of staying out of my cell and chatting with the other leaders in the wing.

We looked out from a window overlooking private houses. The house nearest to us had young teenage girls playing table tennis in the back garden. The way the privileged middle classes occupied their time was in stark contrast to the way we had always lived. We were, of course, envious of their freedom, but more than that their way of life and the love expressed within family bonds.

All the letters we wrote were censored. One day the grey-haired Governor or Chief Officer, who was in sole control of the place, called me to one side as he was walking by with some other officers. He remarked on a word that I had mistakenly put in a letter describing him. I had used the word 'mature' instead of 'distinguished.' He said, *"So you think I am 'mature' do you Farquhar?"* Then, as an afterthought, he said *"As mature as the suns of the desert, eh Farquhar?"* as he walked away with his hands held behind his back - the sign of a wry smile playing on his lips.

Borstal Hewell Grange 1949

I was eventually allocated to a Borstal that was deemed suitable for my make-up and psychological assessment. It was Hewell Grange near Redditch in Worcestershire and an 'Open' one, which meant I was trusted to stay there since it had neither walls nor fence around it. It was a large stately home, once owned by the Paget family. We were taken from Latchmere House by coach; also in transit was a fellow from Manchester called Horridge, who was going back to the Grange after absconding. He was twenty-one with two children and I felt he had let his family down by his actions, something I would never have done - leaving kids without a father - for reasons I mentioned earlier. He did at least tell us what to expect when we got there and was glad to be returning after a spell in a London prison.

Being the new intake, we had to do our first three months scrubbing the stone steps and corridors each day, having first done the twenty-minute morning run at six a.m. in all weathers. We would then have a hot cup of cocoa, before a wash and shave followed by a breakfast of porridge. We would then tidy our room and beds before parading in work parties. We were then counted, before being marched off to either work parties or courses in decorating or bricklaying. I was put on the grounds work party - sawing down old trees and splitting them into six-foot sections suitable for the wood shed, where those on punishments would saw them into logs. This meant sawing with a crosscut which had two bags of sand hanging either end weighing seven pounds each. Though this was punishment of a kind, the culprits on these sessions acquired strong physiques!

I liked what I was doing: it gave me something to think about. I was managing a small team, splitting the trees with eighteen-inch steel wedges that we knocked in with a fourteen-pound hammer, and lopping off branches using a seven-pound axe. I had devised a method of moving the scrubland to be burnt, by shaping branches to carry heavy loads. When it came to splitting large trees, I used shaped wedges made from branches that also helped to free the steel ones when stuck.

On the one occasion my father visited me, we both had to be present while the Governor read my monthly report from my Works Officer, Mr Groves, who stated, *"Farquhar works until he is exhausted and mentions being hungry."* The head was embarrassed to read this in the presence of my father, and asked at what time during the day I felt hungry. I replied *"at lunch time sir!"* He told my father, *"I will make sure he gets some extra food, as he works hard."* The following day I had an extra cob of bread and cheese and this continued all the time I was working on that party.

I enjoyed the wildlife there, especially the birds. They did have a class for birdwatchers, but I was now in the Army Cadets Display Team, practising most nights for that, or doing the usual square bashing - marching to the orders of the ex-army martinets who loved to show off their expertise drilling the squad. One of the housemasters, a Mr Ellvey, who I believe became a Prison Governor, told us a true story about his patrol being in no man's land where there were also enemy patrols on the lookout. They had crawled a fair distance when he saw something shining in the half light, a few yards in front of them. He sent his trusted subaltern to investigate. They heard a faint moan just before he returned to say that it was all clear now. They made their way past the body of a Gestapo officer with his throat cut. From Ellvey's report it was assumed that this 'officer' had placed himself there to check up on his own patrols. It was, Ellvey explained, one of the German ploys to see they were not shirking. What Ellvey had seen was the glint from the full moon on this officer's highly polished boot, and this is what gave him away. This story was told in a whisper, without a sound from the eager group listening. It was worthy of an Oscar.

When it came to education, the time spent at Hewell was a waste of time. Our English teacher was too weak for the lads and the class was a shambles. One evening, a supply teacher from the local grammar school came for two weeks while ours was away. I made myself available, wishing he could be there on a regular basis as I was in awe of him. He was so enthusiastic about his subject that he encouraged us all. The first class was about tenses that I had never learnt; the second about a writer called Thomas Bute, whom he obviously admired. I recall one of his phrases: *"And the man went out into the desert of this world, seating himself down to eat, using his heart as a platter"*

The above are the words he read with such expression and conviction that we could not ignore the genuine feeling he had for it. I am sure that having him as our regular teacher would have benefited me enormously.

I was also moved when a guest speaker came to tell about his experience of running a hostel for the social outcasts of the day, way back in the 1920s. His name was Pop Yates and he spoke of his own poverty as a child and his rule of never refusing a boy admission to his hostel. In consequence, he got the worst of a bad bunch - those who'd been refused places elsewhere. He spoke so movingly of his work and in the end broke down crying, saying how much he hoped we would break the spiral of descent into recidivism. I had never before seen a man cry, so this moved me deeply, as did hearing about what he'd done at the hostel near Ham Common, Richmond.

I was allowed to set rabbit snares around the perimeter fence, and sold most of my catch to the storekeeper, Taffy Williams, who had a large family. This meant I had to run round the fence early, before anyone else could nick them. To achieve this I would have to make sure I was the first one up, drinking my cocoa before the main run then doing the fence run before breakfast.

On one occasion we were taken to see a film called the 'King of Kings' which showed the wonders of the universe in colour. It was a most powerful film. The dialogue informed us about the complexity of the galaxies, and explained how distances within our own galaxy compared with others. It also contained quotes from the Bible, signifying man's relationship with the heavens. It was all done in colour with a powerful musical sound track. We went in small groups to benefit from it.

Being in the Army Cadets Display Team had some rewards, for we went to Tenby in South Wales for a week to have firing range practice and learn to use a Bren gun. There were some young girls there and the fellows went wild over them, exchanging addresses and promising (in subsequent letters) devotion till the end of time. One of my friends met a street photographer he had known back in London: he was down there for the season. He was what was known as a 'West End face' - someone well known, streetwise and able to make money.

I was transferred from the tree-felling party to the best job in the Borstal: that of Officers' Club steward. I had to keep the club tidy and make sure that the coke fire in the bar was lit each day. I also had to arrange things on Wednesdays for the officers' wives afternoon meeting. I would make sure the chairs were placed in such a way that the women's legs would face me while I hid behind the curtain on the stage. One in particular was so attractive she would soon arouse me to the heights of masturbatory passion. At closing time I would clear away their mess and take what cakes were left over to give to the two stokers in the boiler room. The stokers were Vic Pegman from Kilburn and Ron Easterbrook from Deptford. In later life Ron built up a long record and was eventually sentenced for a robbery in Woolwich, where the police waited for the gang to switch cars, then shot some of them. Ron managed to get under a car, thus saving his life. He's been on hunger strike a few times, campaigning to have his case reviewed. He is now in his seventies, still doing time for the crime. I will meet Vic again later in my story. The cakes were well received once a week and made a welcome treat.

I came very near to killing myself one hot summer's day, as I was stoking the large stove with coke until the top was red hot. I began to feel tired, so decided to rest. As I felt ever more tired, I sensed the lack of oxygen in the small room. I crawled along the floor, managing to get some fresh air, and came round with just enough energy to make it out of the place. I quickly refreshed myself with large lungfuls of air. It was a very foolish thing to have done but, no doubt because of my fitness and sense enough to get to the floor, I saved my own life. But it was touch and go.

Soon after my move to the Borstal, I made it my business to become an evening dining-room orderly and got marks from the Housemaster, a decent fellow called Welsford, for volunteering to work around the house. I also realised I would get any food that was left over. I had a chap called Chambers helping me: he was lucky enough to have had a good sex life with his young girlfriend, which made me envious when he related the times they had spent together while her parents were at work. I told him of my experience with the new Medical Officer who, after asking me my name, replied, *"Oh, so you are a silly fucker are you?"* before bursting into laughter at his own joke. I felt angry at hearing this from an adult and was glad to get away from him. Chambers said, *"He did the same thing to me when I told him my name, he said, 'Ha Ha, an old piss pot are you?'"*. We would get plenty of food from the leftovers, so doing the extra duties was well worthwhile, given my appetite.

We all had to go to the local church each Sunday morning. Though it was the most boring time of the day, I do remember reading the fifty-second psalm. *"Thou art shapen into wickedness and in sin hath thy mother conceived thee."* I found this hard to take, once again dismissing the bible and God as bunk, just as I did when I was nine.

Eventually the big day came, only eleven months after leaving Latchmere House - well below the average of eighteen months. I had to talk to the Governor as I

121

walked with him along the drive to the main road. He spoke of my being a loner, not mixing with the other lads; saying how it's a good trait to have in one way but not in others; told me to do my National Service and have a good life, then blessed me as he said goodbye. I was glad I got all the money out without any trouble - there was always a risk of getting caught with it. This was the money I had saved – the profits from selling roll-ups and rabbits during my stay there. I was thankful for this extra money to see me on my way, in addition to the railway pass back too Erith.

It was about this time I read of Joe Purton escaping again, this time with a Polish chap called Stanislaw Zubrouski from Chelmsford Prison. He had taken up the tiles from his cell floor and hidden in a water duct until Zubrouski joined him two days later. The tiles were replaced by an accomplice. They then got away over the wall. Joe was arrested when cornered by the police in Romford sometime later, having been discovered hiding in a flour bin in a bakery. He was sent to Dartmoor where he was to meet up with Bert again, but was in a bad way due to the drugs they had given him to prevent him from re-escaping.

National Service Royal Signals

I did my six weeks' training in Vimy Lines in Catterick under Sergeant Fawcet, following which I was sent to Ripon to be assessed for the type of trade they had in mind for me: I could have been a linesman, radio operator, or despatch rider. I was quite surprised when I saw the officer responsible for allocating army trades. He said they like to keep ex-Borstal boys happy, so what would I like to do? I had heard how the radio operators go mad trying to remember Morse code, so I said, *"Despatch rider please sir."* Bidding him farewell with a sharp salute, I left the room feeling content that I would be doing something which might be useful for future criminal exploits.

In Ripon we lived in what were called 'spiders', with other raw recruits settling down to army trades. One fellow was transferred from the Parachute Regiment to train with us: his name was Smith and was somewhat older, being in the army as a regular. His favourite trick was to get an erection, put a bucket on it, and add a scrubbing brush and broom, then parade around - much to the envy of everyone including myself. It caused much laughter. Smith also gave us examples of how to fall when hitting the ground after jumping from a plane - or how not to fall. This was done by sitting on wooden supports in the roof of the building, before dropping to the floor. I made one attempt and went right through the floorboards, knocking myself up quite a bit. I had no more aspirations of being in his jumping team after that. I was very fit compared to many of the chaps, so when we were in the gym the trainer often told me to watch the others, as I found most of the stuff too easy.

One day, when the sergeant was giving a lecture, he held out a Penguin and slowly unwrapped it, making the class envious of his now exposed chocolate biscuit which he began to eat very slowly, to the envious chuckles of the class. I was rather poker faced during this performance so he asked, *"Don't you find it funny, Farquhar?"* I answered that I didn't find Penguins particularly funny, so he went on with his little ritual and said, *"I do"* as he bit off an extra large piece, much to the joy of the onlookers.

I did try my luck at having a girlfriend: we met at a dance put on for us at a local Church Hall. She lived in Harrogate with her family, one of which was not her real parent. I would walk or part run the seven miles to see her, but I was never lucky enough to have anything more than heavy petting before she would cry. She never made the earth move for me, but nevertheless was of some interest to my emotionally blocked psyche.

I was finding the army somewhat difficult at this time, on account of not having much money, and was toying with the idea of doing a robbery to get some. I soon dropped the girl and went back to stealing. I'd had enough of being broke, so I went into a house near the camp and stole £7 in less than five minutes. Another night I went looking in the Harrogate area, finding a road that had all the hallmarks of good pickings - Pannal Ash Road. I broke into the ground floor lounge of a large crenellated house by taking out a leaded light glass pane. It was big enough to let me get my hand in, to lift the catch to open the larger window. When entering the room, I was overcome by the luxury of the smell of cigar smoke and brandy. I had never come across this before and wondered what I would find elsewhere. The door was locked, so I had to go out the way I came in, determined not to give up but to come back another time with my trusted army knife. I don't know how long I waited before trying again, but the next time I climbed the pipes leading to the bathroom on the top floor. I got into the bathroom, only to find my exit blocked by another locked door. I cut through with my knife - making a hell of a mess but managing to open the door - and found that the key had, stupidly, been left on the other side. Now I had a free run round the whole house. I first tried the master bedroom, which had a safe in its adjoining dressing room. In my search for something valuable, I was unlucky, for even the butler's drinks cabinet was locked. I went back out through the same window I had come in the first time: it saved me scrambling down the wall from the bathroom.

I didn't bother anymore about stealing. I had some leave due, plus extra money for it, so I enjoyed the change and was able to hitch a lift all the way back to London with a fellow called Gardener, who had somehow latched on to me after a fight I had with a Scottish chap. I was now trying hard to get a posting to Whitehall, which was the best place to be at the time. I asked to see a Captain Booth, to arrange a compassionate posting on the grounds that I was the only breadwinner in the family and would like to be near them in London. I told him of my plight and, though he gave me little hope, he was sympathetic to my situation and said that had it been up to him I would have been given the posting without a doubt.

One day, on a slow ride over the Yorkshire Dales, negotiating the twists and turns in the road, we stopped for a problem up ahead because blasting was taking place, near some high ground to my right. I immediately took down the map reference, realising this was where I could get explosives when the time came. I felt elated at this piece of information, feeling my ambition was at last coming to fruition.

Most of the recruits I did my training with had been posted to various parts of the world. I made myself known to the postings clerk in the office in the hope of getting a place in the London area as a favour to me. On one occasion, as I was going over the moors in winter, a slight smattering of snow appeared on the way up to Catterick HQ - but on the return journey I was travelling in deep snow, miles from any sign of habitation. Then the bike broke down, refusing to start again. I was very cold by now, so decided to warm my gloved hands round the engine. I had to pull them away quickly after the initial sizzling, as they burnt a little, then realised they had crinkled around the palms and fingers. I then pushed my fingers deeper into the gloves, at the same time folding my fingers up into a fist, and felt the gloves disintegrate, exposing my bare hands without any covering. I cursed my stupidity, having a broken down bike in the middle of nowhere, freezing cold with gloves not now suitable for anything, due to my own stupid actions. I tried to get the thing started and it was a hard job taking off the petrol feed to the carburettor in order to release any muck that may have done the damage. It worked and I was soon glad to get out of the place, holding the handlebars with the gauntlet part of the gloves, partially keeping the cold wind out of my near frozen hands. There were times while crossing that moor when I realised that the telephone poles should have been on my right instead of left making me aware of the fact I had left the road and was travelling literally on the moor. I still made it back, thankfully with all despatches safe and sound.

The time came when world events affected our comfortable existence at Ripon, and standing orders declared that all personnel without postings were to report the following morning, in full FSMO, ready to go to No. 1 Training Depot. I reported late, wearing an overcoat and carrying all my belongings in a kitbag. I was then ushered into a waiting lorry, out of sight of the Military Police office, for not being properly dressed. I felt let down at having to go aboard when my plans were finally coming to fruition, as I had found a good place to obtain explosives. We were all transported to the Training Depot for embarkation to various parts of the world, but in hindsight I realised it could have been the new hotspot, Korea. We were all assembled in one room and asked who was not willing to go abroad. My hand came up immediately. I was the only one willing to appear a coward - or perhaps the bravest. I was asked why I didn't want to go and replied that it was personal and that I would like to see an officer. I saw both the O.C. and the C.O. at different times; giving the same reason I had given previously to Captain Booth, that I was the only breadwinner in the family. The C.O. said, *"Soldier on laddy; have your leave; put your things with the Quartermaster until you return."*

I placed my kit in the stores, as instructed, and was given the number thirty-two and told not to forget it. I never returned. I had the leave at home with my mother and then went to see my father, who arranged for me to stay with him at his digs, which turned out to be with one of the top crime families of S.E. London. I fitted in with his way of life, for he worked close by in a factory as a storeman.

I soon made contact with my old friend, and went back to committing the usual small- time crimes which gave us the money to live from. One day R introduced me to a fellow who wanted to join up with us. He was older and said he knew my mother well, as it was he who had got her cousin Israel away from the coach on the day they had sawn the cuffs off at our house. When I heard his name I soon put two and two together, realising he'd been involved in one of the most infamous of crimes committed soon after the end of the war. It was the '*de Annquise*' murder, where two ex-Borstal boys tried to hold up '*Jays*' the jewellers in Tottenham Court Road. The alarm was set off as they made their escape through the traffic, but they didn't take into account the public spiritedness of the ex-sailor, Mr. de Annquise, the father of six children. One or other of the two crooks, Jerehety or Jenkins, shot him dead as he drove his motorcycle at them, preventing their escape.

Lordy, our new-found friend, whose real name was Bill Welsh, got his nickname when going over the Marsh giving out sixpences to the young travelling kids who asked him for money. A sixpence, in rhyming slang, was known as a 'tanner', corrupted from a Lord of the Manor. He was no doubt involved in the robbery as look out, and had panicked when he saw it all go wrong, managing nevertheless to hide a raincoat and bag-wash sack which had a number indelibly printed on it. A top-ranking detective called Fabian was assigned the task of catching the villains responsible for this man's untimely death.

There was a public outcry, which brought to light the articles hidden in the toilets of an office block near where the crime had been committed. It wasn't long before the bag was identified and traced to someone in the Woolwich area, who had given it to Lordy. The two were soon apprehended and, while on remand in Brixton Prison, spoke to my father who was in there for not paying maintenance to my mother. He said they were in good cheer and willing to talk to anyone during exercise periods. I have no reason to disbelieve my father, as he wouldn't lie on a matter such as that. They were both hanged.

Lordy did some crimes with R, realising he had skills that neither of us had. After a time, he told us he could blow a safe, so it was up to Settle to get the explosives. We hired a car from Grants in Woolwich and Lordy drove there, as neither of us could drive. We found my map reference easily, but had trouble finding the right shed amongst the many there. Lordy said we should find the one with the lightning conductor on it. Presto, he was right. We then stocked up with what we needed, taking only slow burning fuses - the kind you see in cowboy films. That same night we blew the safe in a cinema at Harrogate, getting just over £400, which suited us well enough for a first attempt. Lordy took the car back, while R and I went back in style from Leeds station, having first had a good clean up with hot towels in a barber.

I had now achieved my ambition of being a safe blower, but did not once think of my family or others. I gambled and drank with my father, going with the women from Hyde Park at night when I had need of them. My father would be with one against a tree and I another, depending on how I felt, with the perverts who walked round the couples at the same time masturbating. I would get annoyed and go for them, half- drunk, angered by their continual circling. I was nineteen, England's youngest safe blower, and responsible for organising most of the crimes we committed. As I couldn't trust Lordy, I gave my address to R who would call when money was tight: we would then choose a cinema or another target between us. Lordy was always ready to do something, as he gambled heavily. I arranged to hide the explosives somewhere near the proposed cinema, say under the dustbins at the rear, so as not to jeopardise our chances by getting caught with explosives before they were needed. Once, when waiting to join the queue to go into a cinema somewhere in the north of England, Lordy took off his hat and said, *"They might just as well come over here and put it in my effing hat 'cos we'll get it tonight anyway"* which we did - with such consummate ease.

Another time we arranged to do a Post Office. I was expecting to see just R, but he had turned up with the chap I hadn't forgotten from my childhood over the wellie episode, when I was asked to run to see how fast I was. This was the same fellow who, when he was sixteen, was given a job that required him to have a shotgun. I was getting some conkers by throwing sticks for them when this same chap fired the bloody thing at a shed close to me, expecting me to run away frightened. But I had stood my ground and carried on getting the things until he fired again, when I told him to pack it up as I wasn't going to go. I told both of them, in strong language, what a liberty they had taken and that what we were doing was not a fucking peep show or circus and for the other c... to fuck off and get out of it lively.

It all went well enough from then on, doing what had to be done. Though little money was taken, it was enough to make it worthwhile. The other chap said he had come along to watch and wanted nothing out of it.

I couldn't believe R's stupidity. To some degree I was like Pinky in Brighton Rock - a young man still in his teens with a completely disturbed psyche dedicated to crime. I was on the run from the army for twenty-one months in all, occasionally doing some form of work when I needed a rest from crime or when I felt vulnerable. But work didn't last for long.

I tried the Festival of Britain, arranging with my father to get me the job. He was doing well enough selling tea from a stall, doing his usual 'one for me one for you' routine. I only lasted two hours washing dishes.

One day, Lordy arranged with me to do the cinema at Hayes near Bromley. We didn't do the usual thing, like stowing the explosives and tools for breaking in at the back of the cinema. Instead we holed up in a garden shed at the back of a house not far from the High Street – stupid, but we took a chance. I had a chat with Lordy about his family learning that he had a son from a previous marriage way back. I never thought of him having a family, nor did I want to know in those days. After all, we more or less worked as contractors, each of us doing his bit. We smoked and chatted until two in the morning, then made our move along the darkened road leading to the town. Suddenly a patrol car swerved round the corner, catching us both in its headlights. I dived under a low wall about twenty inches high - just enough to cover me while I was busy burying the explosives and torch. By now, Lordy had been apprehended and was sitting above me, smoking a cigarette given to him by one of the coppers who was asking him where the other chap had gone. The rest of the crew were searching gardens further along the road, shining torches everywhere but towards me as I huddled close to the wall, my heart beating like a pile driver and Lordy's cigarette coming very near to poking me in the eye as he flicked the ash off.

After a time they gave up looking, taking away their captive, glad no doubt that they had had success of a kind. I stayed there for an hour in case they had left someone at the bottom of the road to watch out for me. I'd previously noticed trains going by the top of the road, so I made my way there, walking along the line until I came across a workman's hut with a place I could make a fire. I was quite cold by now, so I waited until six, then caught a train from New Cross Station back to central London where I was sharing a flat with a fellow I had met in Borstal. He was living with Jessie, a prostitute who worked Hyde Park and the Great West Road, picking up lorry drivers. I was later told that she would occasionally, unknown to me, bring her clients back to the flat.

While I was living there, I met an Irish girl who worked in a pub near the Brompton Oratory. She asked to come back to the flat with me after I took her to the fair on Hampstead Heath. As I have mentioned earlier, getting involved with a woman was the last thing on my mind and I did not want the problems that this would bring. My father had to tell me she was after me, as I knew nothing of the opposite sex at all. There were times when I was with a prostitute that I had a yearning to say *"I love you,"* when deeply involved with sex. I had one tall woman who I would sometimes sleep with regularly. She was always pleased to see me when I picked her up on her beat off Bond Street: she would take me back to a friend's place, eager for me to sleep with her. She never bothered about taking money from me - it was done as an afterthought, as I left it on the mantelpiece.

Lordy phoned a few days later in quite high spirits, saying all they had on him was carrying housebreaking implements by night. He didn't have a torch - I was holding that – but he did have gloves, a tap wrench and rose bit, which saved him carrying a large brace and bit. He phoned one more time, before being remanded in custody, and was eventually sent to the sessions, getting seven years' Preventive Detention. Once they had checked him out, and knowing of his association with the de Annquise case, they didn't hold back with vilifying his character, such as 'associating with known criminals in South East London' and 'failing to assist the police by giving them the name of the person with him at the time of his capture'. Although Lordy got a bad deal on paper (so to speak), I wonder whether, looking back over his influence on both Roy and myself, he was somehow getting what he deserved in the scheme of things. Is there an arbiter, responsible for another form of justice? Lordy was no doubt meant to be caught that night, leaving me free to obtain my inevitable sentence.

R and I and I did another cinema together then called it a day, knowing it would only be a matter of time before our luck ran out, since the police were keeping a special watch on cinemas, particularly those in the Home Counties. There were times when we had lucky escapes, with the police entering the buildings while we were still in them, prior to breaking into the office. I stole some drink and cigarettes from a pub in Slades Green, Kent. It happened that a relative had been arrested and charged with receiving them, so I thought I would do another cinema to get some help for him. I was caught, and glad in a way to end this disturbed, stressful existence.

I was caught in Surrey, so I went to Guildford Quarter Sessions and was sentenced to eighteen months on two charges, to run concurrently. I thought I'd got three years but was elated when they told me I would be out in a year's time, not understanding the difference between 'concurrent' and 'consecutive'. I vowed I would never commit any serious crimes again, aware at last that I had a lot of catching up to do with the life that I had missed by sublimating my natural drives that way.

Lewes Prison 1952

I went to Lewes Young Offenders' Prison in Sussex with something of a reputation, a result I suppose of the judge telling the court that, *"In all my time on the bench, now in my eightieth year, I have never met anyone as young, as mature in the art of crime as you Farquhar."* I took a painting and decorating course while I was there, getting 95% marks for practical work and theory. A fellow called Williams had similar marks. I took an intelligence test with another chap called Josephs and we both had marks above average.

It was my first introduction to any form of knowledge. I was allowed to have my light on for an hour later than the other prisoners, but I would read rather than eat. When I was given books by the Education Tutor, a man named Powell for whom I have the deepest regard, he offered me the chance to spend my time usefully, in study. Nothing was too much for him. He wore a khaki safari jacket in the summer months: it distinguished him from the Prison Service and accentuated his eccentricity.

It was here that I first realised my ignorance. I sipped a little from the Pirian Spring, whetting my appetite in wonder at the masters. My first book was on Practical Ethics, and led me to another language, requiring a dictionary to help me grasp the ideas of the writer. It was hard going but most enjoyable, breaking through concepts in my puny, ignorant mindset: *"The lover will go to the end of the earth for his love. How far will the lover of wisdom go?"* I first came across this quote in 1953.

One evening I was told to give some pens out to the class and, when I had finished, was asked which pen I had kept for myself. Even though there were new ones amongst them, the tutor was surprised that I hadn't kept one of them for myself. I didn't think about it at the time and would not have given it another thought, had he not brought it to my attention. How would he have reacted if he had known I was in prison for helping someone in a jam?

On arrival at Lewes I met Vic Pegman, the stoker I had given cakes to with Ron Easterbrook back at Hewell Grange. He was pleased to see me and asked what landing and cell I was in. He worked in the kitchen and put a cob and butter in for me each day. I got it for about a week, but then it disappeared. I suspected the cleaner of taking it so I got Vic to lock the door. The cleaner later killed two young teenage girls in what was to be known as the Tow Path Murders: his name was Whiteway.

The axe he used was stolen by one of the squad car drivers who, having seen it in the shed, took it home for his own use. He later confessed to putting it in the boot of his car and forgetting it was there. Vic had been involved in a fight on Kilburn High Road and had knifed someone, a crime for which he received four years. Ron Easterbrook is still fighting his case, claiming that the villains had fired first after the police in Woolwich shot up the gang he was with. The police had been tipped of by an informant about where the gang were planning to change cars after a robbery. The robbery was dubbed the *'old age pensioners' crime'* because Ron was in his late fifties at the time.

I had a visit from my father and my brother Bob, plus his latest woman whom he left outside to wait. I was pleased to see my brother: he looked so much like a younger version of Elvis Presley - very fit as he neared his sixteenth birthday. All was going well until my half-drunk father began to say stupid things about the officer seated nearby. I thought how foolishly he was behaving, and told the officer to take me back to the wing, but not before scolding my father for acting as he had done in front of my brother, setting him a bad example by acting like a bloody kid himself. He shouted an apology to me as I was led out of the room and taken on exercise. I began to talk to the two fellows in front of me about my row on the visit, when an officer told me to get further away from those in front. I snapped, telling him to fuck off and not to piss me off. I thought I was going to get marched off and slung down the chokey hole for what I had done, but nothing happened, just another reiteration of his first request for me to get back away from those in front. I could only assume that word had perhaps got round when they had to put me back on exercise, that I had

had a rough time on the visit. It was a very tough nick to be in and the slightest infringement of the rules was met with punishment, like chokey for three days on bread and water, no mattress in the cell all day, and nothing to read except perhaps a book on gardening.

A couple of months before my release I had a letter from my father saying that he would send me a hundred pounds because he had won the pools and had a cheque for two thousand quid. Soon after the letter I got photos of him in some nightspot or other with a young girl by his side, drooling over him as they imbibed the various drinks on show at their table. I did get £30, and this was very handy because when I got out three months later he had gone through the lot, plus another five hundred on top which he had won racing.

The night I came out we went to the West End to the same drinking hole he had been frequenting for the last three months. My flat-share character from Borstal asked me, *"Who's the fellow you're with Ron? He's been coming down here treating the band to play happy birthday every two weeks."* The photographs he sent me were scattered around the cell, attracting the officers who were keen to see what it was like to have such young women on your arm at forty. My father made a mistake when he tried to date our ex-landlady's daughter – she was the partner of a well-known villain who was doing twelve years for his part in the London Airport robbery. He got a good hiding that quietened him down for a while: it was no doubt mentioned that he'd sponged from me in the past. He never did anything for me as a father: I was too strong a character anyway.

Before I left Lewes, I had a visit from an army sergeant and two corporals, asking what had happened to my uniform and clothing that I had left at the Quartermaster's store. It was a courtesy visit to say they were not proceeding with any charges. They also asked me why I had deserted and got me to sign for clothing that had gone astray. I said I thought I was just a number in the army, along with some other observations that didn't go down with the top brass: I was discharged with ignominy.

Back to Erith 1953

Going back to Erith, I joined the library and enrolled at Woolwich Technical College for adult classes in wood graining, adding to what I already knew about decorating. Marbling was also part of the course. I found my first girlfriend, Margaret, but haven't any recollection of our first meeting except that we had planned to get engaged - much to the ire of her parents - but I got cold feet as the plans were being laid for an engagement party. I realised I had a lot more to do in life, having missed out on my teenage years, and I felt the need to catch up on so much. So, at the last moment, I called it off - just when she had most of the plans arranged. I went with Margaret to the Embassy Ballroom in Welling on one occasion, but felt like a leper amongst the dancers enjoying themselves. I had bouts of alienation, feeling a weight on my shoulders that stopped me from mixing and enjoying life.

Prior to going steady (as the saying went) with Margaret, I used to go out on the booze with Bert and Roy, his brother in law. Once, as we were waiting on the crowded platform at Woolwich Arsenal Station for our train home, we exchanged some words with a fellow kissing his girlfriend on the opposite platform. He responded in kind and before long a slanging match blew up between us. I soon had enough of this and jumped down onto the railway line, ran across, and knocked him out for his trouble. As I ran back out of the entrance, I met his mate on the way up the stairs. I quickly told him that someone had hit his friend, and then ran to a side entrance on the platform I had been on earlier, catching the train as it pulled out, cock-a-hoop at what I had done.

Margaret later told me she had seen everything that took place, as one of the crowd on the platform, and was in agreement with my action, saying he deserved it for his attitude. This was the first of my psychotic actions that, in hindsight, I can describe as utter madness. I was to act the same way later, again when drunk. Maybe Margaret agreed with my action because, at her young age, she had never before experienced anything quite as violent, and was perhaps thrilled to have been part of it in some strange way.

I attended the evening classes for nine months, until I met an old school friend who introduced me to a pub that sold cheap cider. It was here that I met some of the characters from Woolwich, who could have come out of Steinbeck's *'Cannery Row'*. One was to be my friend for many years: I dubbed him James 'Aloysius' Thorne. It seemed to suit him, being so enigmatic, never knowing how he would behave from one moment to the next. He was a great comic, who could bring tears to your eyes with his weird sense of humour. On other occasions, if he found something not quite to his liking, you had to stand clear - or connect with his right hand. I had many a good time with Jim, letting of steam, making up for my confused background: I was never comfortable with ordinary people and my alienation was hard to live with. Going to dances was most difficult, even when under the influence of drink: it didn't work for me. There were times I would go into the toilets to hold my head in despair, unable to enjoy myself as others around me were doing.

I tried dancing classes, and on both occasions a middle-aged gay tutor took me as a partner - much to my dislike. The other place was in New Cross. This also proved to be a waste of time, and I stopped going after three attempts because the fellow running it was a twenty-five year-old Italian who had eighteen partners eagerly waiting for him to take on the floor. What chance did I and any another male novice have, in the face of this set up? I went for three nights after work, perhaps to have a chance with one of the girls - but no hope, with that smooth-talking, dark, six-foot-something, bloody good looking Italian behaving like a Chanticleer to his adoring Pertelotes.

My two Borstal friends met up with me to do a crime and, too stupid to refuse, I led them on a long walk with some old gelignite that had been kept hidden in a wall in a front room along with some detonators for a year or more. It was in a state, sweating a lot and in my opinion useless, but the police would not have known that. I was more than half hearted about it so gave up after one night doing nothing.

Time at Sea

After a while I decided to work on a ship, so I trained in Newcastle to become a stoker. I went there with a fellow from Bexleyheath called Charlie Swan. We both stood outside offices in Newcastle centre, causing girls to look out of windows at the way we were dressed, as we wore overcoats with wide shoulders that made an impression on those fashion-conscious Geordie females. We were being treated like film stars for that short time, waving to them all as we wallowed in their adoration: I loved the Geordie people and their friendliness. Once, when we were there to commit crimes, we asked a fellow the way to a certain area. Five minutes later, panting and out of breath from running to catch us up, he said he'd directed us the wrong way!

My first trip to sea was quite an experience, wresting thirty-foot waves across the Atlantic To St Johns, New Brunswick. Where I watched stevedores unload the cargo far quicker than our British counterparts, whom I saw wait and think about it before attempting to move anything. I was also impressed by the way mature women looked with well coiffed hair dressed so smartly compared with our English equivalents, who looked like peasants in the mid- fifties. Most were on their way to play housey -housey. Our later equivalent of Bingo, yet to reach our shores.

The SS Maplecove was a dry ship (one where drink is not allowed) nine thousand tons with reinforced steel hatches to withstand the Atlantic crossings. So when we berthed at Antwerp all hell broke loose among the crew. I went on another psychotic bender causing another crew member to do three months in a Belgian prison. I later learned that this was the result of my fighting a man in a club and pulling a chandelier from the ceiling in a brothel. The captain had to stand bail for the rest of the crew to get them out of the local prison and police station to catch the morning tide back to England.

My last trip was to Jamaica. The sea this time was so calm you could have followed behind in a canoe. I had the most depressing work on this ship the Ebro owned by the Royal Mail Line. My job was in the engine room, cleaning out oil that congealed into a fatty substance after being preheated before firing the furnace through six jets under high pressure. I could never see myself doing this form of work with those great pistons propelling us forward night and day. I could write of the crew and the journey out, but there would be nothing to say except that it was not a happy ship. I didn't get on very well with the engineer, for some reason, Perhaps he just didn't fit into my good' guy book'. I managed to leave the boat in Jamaica on medical grounds. On the first night off the ship I lost fifteen pounds from my sock as I was sleeping with a woman. It was a lot to lose, so had to be careful with the £30 I had left. In the kitty.

I saw a lot of poverty there. When a local store advertised nineteen vacancies for the Spring Sales, five hundred people applied. They had to call out the riot police in large numbers to quell the crowd. Kids would walk barefoot behind you, dart their small hands in your pockets and take what they could grab before you knew what was happening. Everybody made out they knew the cook on the ship and would ask for a shilling from you. I had the quick hand down the trousers one night. This was done by a fellow my age and he fell to the ground as I turned. I screamed obscenities at him, and was threatening to kick him when two of his friends came out from the shadows, also barefoot, and the uglier and tougher-looking of the two had a knife that he held to my throat saying, *"You keeck, you keeck, you keeck."* I somehow mumbled out some excuse, *"I haven't got any money and all the people round here know me as 'Beachy' 'cos I'm waiting for my ship to get back."* I stared at him eye to eye, waiting for him to move, thinking I would then kick him hard in the shins and run. He slowly took the knife away and I ambled off for a short way before breaking into a run until I got back to the Mission, knocking up the caretaker and jumping through the top of the stable door as quick as I could, moaning about his countrymen trying to rob me.

In the second week of my stay I was taken by taxi to an unknown destination: the driver wouldn't say where he was taking me. As we headed further out from Kingston, I began to feel apprehensive. After about forty minutes I noticed fields with barbed wire covering the tops of the fences. People working in the fields looked at us as we turned down a dirt road. I began to feel uneasy. Was this a mental institution of some kind and was I going to have my mental state assessed because I'd told the company doctor I had feelings of depression and suicide? I had made a bet to get off the ship with another toe rag who wouldn't work if he could avoid it. I felt *"well this is it Farquhar, you've put yourself into a bloody situation now."* I was taken to see the psychiatrist, a Mr Capoore, who asked me what type of work I had on the ship, what I did before joining the Merchant Navy and why I joined in the first place. I answered, *"As a way to see the world"*. After a few more questions he said, *"It seems that you are a square peg in a round hole, Mr Farquhar. You can go back to the Mission and I shall send my report to the company in due course."* I couldn't get back quick enough, elated at not having to stay in the place.

My remaining time was spent with the sexually liberated women in Jamaica who liked the idea of having a white baby. I met a woman of twenty-one who had three children sleeping in the same makeshift bed we used. She was half Indian, which gave her a likeness to a Trechikov painting, with high cheekbones and large brown eyes. I met two Spanish fellows who were waiting to be deported back to Franco's Spain for being communists. We visited the same living space-*cum*-dancing area each night. The better looking and more outgoing of the Spanish guys was staying with one of the women, as grateful as I was to have a partner each night. My partner told me that her friend had asked her what she saw in me, and she had replied, *"He romances me nice."* I must admit I did like the sexual freedom, completely natural and without the hang-ups you would have from European women worried about the consequences of children. I feel indebted to this black beauty, who called me her 'Errol Flynn' - I had a moustache then. She also noticed that when I walked I twisted my wrist behind me. I never had received such attention from a woman before, nor so much sexual freedom. When the boat returned to Kingston I had to go back on board. I reluctantly said goodbye to my Trechikov companion, missing the sex but grateful for the time we had spent together and for the way she had given her body to me with such passion, never once asking for money the whole time I was with her.

Back on the ship I was given a real stinker of a job, scraping the carbon from inside the piston sleeves with the flat end of a file. The heat was well over a hundred degrees so I wore nothing but jeans, drinking plenty of barley water every twenty minutes. I did it for two days and was glad when it finished - the hardest work I'd done in my life. On the way home I sat at the stern of the ship, watching the white ribbon of the wash made by the propellers, as the sunset vanished, leaving the lights of the blue mountain slowly disappearing below the waves. I thought of the thousands of men who'd left their homeland to make a new life in other parts of the world, as they may have watched their country descend beneath the waves in the night, fearful of never seeing their homeland again. I felt a deep affinity with them at the time, within that hour or more, as I watched the island descend below the horizon, knowing I would never see the place again.

I was soon back home with the drinking partners of Woolwich, eager to pick up where I'd left off six months previously. I had only been back a week, when I was invited to a party at Charlton. All went well, with Jim now married to Joyce, the woman he had met while lying on the floor of the Oak pub after being knocked about in a fight. Staring through booze-glazed eyes, he must have thought her some angel, dispensing honeyed unction to his blood- spattered face. Jim, always the joker, made the party go with a bang, doing his spoons act to all the Mums, eager to take my cigarettes, knowing I'd been to Jamaica and was still in the Merchant Navy.

Two girls left so I decided to try and catch up with them by borrowing a motorbike without the owner knowing. But I came a cropper, hitting an electric junction box which governed all the lights in the road. A large blue flame came from it as I somersaulted over to land in the middle of the road, minus my right shoe which had been wrenched off on impact. I saw a low wall to my right and crawled for it, hoping to hide behind it. But I hadn't allowed for shock, which made me shake uncontrollably. The next I remembered was a voice saying, *"Here's his shoe"* as it bounced along the floor of the ambulance - into oblivion.

The next day I woke in St Nick's Hospital, Plumstead with a dry mouth and a swollen right knee, but otherwise glad to be alive. My friend Jim came with Joyce to see the wild idiot who was to end up in there for ten days, much to the annoyance of the local police. Jim called again some days later, thoughtfully bringing me some motorcycle magazines that he said, *"Would help me with reading matter."* He was always very helpful when it came to choosing the right gifts! He included a cutting from the local paper, which reported how lucky a motorcyclist had been when he collided with the junction box in Charlton Road and was nearly killed by 40,000 volts. The police charged me for stealing the bike, and I was taken to the police station with my worldly goods in a carrier bag. I asked if I could leave them at the station, but they said, *"No, you had better take them".* They knew best, for I was placed before a small, receding, grey-haired magistrate wearing bi-focal spectacles which made him look like a clone of Lord Douglas-Hume. As he peered through them at me, with a penetrating weasel-like stare, he asked if I had anything to say. I foolishly said, *"I was drunk, Sir."* He then went off into the closest thing to a paroxysmal fit I have ever seen in my life, repeating the word, "Drunk!", "drunk!" before rattling off a jumble of words that eluded my, by now, befuddled brain. I descended the stairs to await transport to Wandsworth, having receiving five months and myriad added appendices concerning no insurance, no driving licence, being drunk, without due care and attention and the like, as well as causing damage to property. I had the sentence explained to me by the copper, as he was waiting to document me before the meat wagon picked me up. I was now twenty-three years old and living as I had more or less planned when in Lewes Prison, except I was missing the right social skills. I had tried dancing but somehow could not mix with the opposite sex. My feelings of alienation were still a problem, as I tried to live down a broken home and army desertion, as well as, perhaps depression. They all combined to make me feel of no value to anyone, or society. At the time, of course, I was not aware of the reason for these feelings, not having been fortunate enough to have had any type of therapy.

I remember little of the five months in Wandsworth, other than having a fight and getting three days' bread and water in the choky cells. This was given by the notorious Governor Lawton, who'd come up through the ranks. I was doing the cleaning on the landing, when I had a literal head-on collision with a well known 'face' from the West End, who was learning the basics of Martial Arts which were just starting to be practised in this country. I'd never heard the word 'Karate' before he told me about it while hardening the sides of his hands by continually pounding them against the wall behind him. He was known as 'Scouse Ted' and thought himself a good speller, showing off while waiting in the serving area by spelling the word 'Ecclesiastical' to the rest of us.

One day, after collecting the food from the kitchen, he stood behind the sweet container holding the ladle which I needed for my job. I asked him for it and he threw it towards me saying, *"Stick it up your fucking arse."* I hit him with my head, at the same time kneeing him in the groin - aware of the possibility of his hardened palms chopping my neck and body had I not moved first. I'd come a long way since being head-butted at fifteen by Taffy Davis in the hostel at Forest Gate. Ted's ability to spell didn't help him on that occasion. I hope you fared well in life, Ted.

I was transferred to D Wing where long timers were housed. From reading the cards on their doors, I noticed that many were doing life. I had a cell on my own and worked in the sewing shop sweeping the floors of cotton waste. I was approached by some of the fellows to do those favours, such as seeing their friends or relatives when I got out, as word was soon on the grapevine that I was a short timer. One fellow, known as the king of parcel thieves, asked me to start up again for him while he was away. He upset another chap in the workshop, who subsequently waited until he was in the recess and smashed his china mug in his face while he bent to get some water. It was a severe blow, doing quite a bit of damage: the assailant was known as Whitey. I was released in time to go hop picking with my mother and Joe. We took along my brother Bob who was on the run from Feltham Borstal; my aunts Mary and Emma were also there. All was well until the police came to see a fellow about the road tax on his car. Unaware of this, my aunt Mary said something about Bob being wanted by the police, but she was overheard by one of the local women measuring her hops. Later that day the police came back in full force, going straight to our hut where our Alsatian dog Sally put her hackles up, baring her teeth at the now very angry copper who was asking where my brother was. Realising that he wasn't getting anywhere and had little chance of searching the hut, he said, *"OK if that's the way you want it, we'll get our own dogs."* With that, they all foolishly went away without leaving a copper to wait and watch out if anyone came from the hut. When they came back, Bob was long gone. When my mother saw the eight dogs on leads plus a bloodhound, she broke down, crying uncontrollably at the sight of her son being hunted down like an animal, in such a way.

Was it necessary for him to do what he did just to apprehend an eighteen year-old escapee from a Borstal while his mother looked on? All this took place because a police chief had little or no respect for people that he regarded as beneath him. Did it really warrant that action? I am sure he over-reacted in the same way the police did when one of their marksmen killed the chap 'Poole'. One thing that did occur in my favour was that the police action was witnessed by a rather attractive woman. She was very sympathetic for the wrong done to our family and gave herself to me, out of compassion and love for another human being. Her feminine emotion of caring was expressed so passionately. She stayed with me for two nights, sharing the intimacy of her body and the beauty of the natural world as we walked together in the warm Autumnal moonlight. I compared this episode to the one experienced by the ex-con McVicar who, when giving a talk on sociology, was given sex freely by a young undergraduate after learning he had not had sex for seven years. She did it for the joy of doing it, in an act of pure altruism.

Bob did come back later, and made his way to other friends after getting money from my mother. I went back to Erith for a while, selling various things door-to-door that I had bought from a firm called Fredrick Winners, dealers in bankrupt stock in the Farringdon Road. It was hard going, but I preferred it in the summer to painting and decorating.

I then thought it would be worthwhile to try working on a fairground where I could meet plenty of those young girls who like hanging around when it comes to town. I wrote to an address in the *'Worlds Fair'*, a paper read by many travelling fairground people. I was taken on by a major operator, Roses, and went to live at their winter quarters in Hounslow, doing odd jobs until the season started a month or so later in the spring. I was now twenty-four. The first place we pulled into was Hampton Court, where a special gang of locals did the work of putting up and pulling down while others were taken on for the job of collecting money. The living conditions were rough, with just a blanket to cover you at night in a dirty bunk of sorts. I was asked to look after a young fellow, whose parents were both music hall artistes. They wanted their sixteen-year-old son to rough it, just as they had, to toughen him up a little. Needless to say, I only stayed on for perhaps two other places as I got fed up with not finding any girls. I didn't like feeling bloody dirty all the time and I resented having the responsibility of looking after the other young fellow. Soon after this I went back to London.

I had little money and few clothes, although I still had the overcoat that had caused all the fuss in Newcastle. It was a dark blue doeskin made by Charkham's in Tottenham Court Road, purchased back in the safe blowing days of 1952.

I had to find a cheap place to stay on the quick, so I went to a Rowton House, one of many to be found in London. I went to the one in Hammersmith, as this was the nearest to my father and brother John's digs in Acton. It was also near to Fulham Broadway, where building workers could cash in their holiday stamps. I had some, which would help to tide me over for a while. I had never been to a place like this, but decided to have a go at it, too proud to sponge on my mother and Joe. I had to queue to book a bed the very same afternoon that I left the fair. My next visit was to the Labour Exchange (as it was then known), where I got a job as a decorator, starting the very next day. I was given a token to secure me a bed for the night. I looked out of place compared to those waiting with me, their scruffy appearance contrasting with my expensive doeskin coat. In the evening I was shown the cubicle, and settled down to sleep after securing my trousers under the mattress, along with the little money I had left.

I spread my overcoat over the bed, gripping it tight around the collar, and eventually went to sleep after the noise of the singing drunks quietened down around three in the morning. I was disturbed in the night by a slight tug on the overcoat. I relaxed a little, but the same thing happened again. This time I became aware of more tugging, before the coat went off the bed, onto the floor, then out of the door, carried by a bare-footed, grey-haired man who was hot-footing along the long corridor then out through the swinging doors at the end. I had to run, tripping over the jerry pot and upsetting the contents over the floor, cursing all the time for the bastard to drop it before he disappeared. I continued cursing all the way down to the office, where a night porter, disturbed from his sleep, commiserated with my loss and outburst of language saying that the overcoat will be found in the quadrangle in the morning for sure. He was right: it was indeed there, but minus the stamps I had been relying on to keep me until I found digs and deposit, before I got my first wage.

I went on a job paperhanging, then off the next day with the usual mixture of painters - some better than others but all good fellows. The foreman was a decent chap called Gunner, who knew some of the local villains. One had arranged to work on our team soon after me, so he could say he had a regular job when he appeared in court for running a 'spieler' (a place for illegal gambling). The chap in question had never done a day's work in his life, but it would go well in his favour in court if he had a job. I told Gunner my story about the overcoat going off the bed and was given a sub to help me get digs. I found a place off the Fulham Palace Road with a mature couple named Weiss, who were very helpful when they learned of my work as a painter: they then gave me small jobs that helped towards the rent.

While I was there I wrote to 'lonely hearts' columns, looking in the main for single parents as I reasoned that a woman with a child wouldn't mind knowing a person with a criminal record: we could bond as outsiders, both socially alienated as illegitimacy was at the time. I had a reply from a girl in Dagenham and met her a few times, but I wasn't attracted to her in any way, other than through loneliness and her beauty. I had done a good job of sublimating my sexual drives, for I couldn't free myself from the mindset that I had about women when I was a criminal. I wanted to get back to some normal way of living, not feel tainted by my background. I bought some powdered clay in an attempt to sculpt her face from memory: she had such a wonderful bone structure. The last time I saw her, she had taken a live-in job in a pub in Southampton. Some years later, while working as an industrial painter, I came across a chap who said he'd recognised me walking the same girl with fabulous legs in an area of scrubland in Dagenham.

I stayed long enough to get back on my feet, but had a disagreement with Gunner and left, getting digs in Acton near my brother John and father. This was to be an important juncture in my life, breaking from the depression and allowing natural joy into my life after such a long time. I found the young landlady very attractive, no doubt because of my new found energy in finding work locally as a decorator, and visiting both my brother and father for drinking sessions. I made an impression on this young mother of two girls and her husband Eddie. Irma was a very attractive, tall blonde with a slim figure that cracked my indifference towards women. I had a desire for this beauty that broke the shell I had hidden behind for too long. I was also going back to Woolwich and meeting up with the bold Jim Thorne and one or two others of the Cannery Row characters. All good fun while the beer flowed and Jim would either act the clown or look for a fight with someone he didn't like. Jim Butterfield, an ex-Air Force National Serviceman and I had many a good night together. I was now making up for my time spent in the institutions of my early youth: I had somewhere to live and a good family to share my life with.

Later, I stole motorcycles to get myself back to Acton, much the worse for drink. I managed never to get caught 'borrowing' them. It was before the time when you had to wear a crash helmet, so I avoided getting stopped in the early hours going through traffic lights. I made some fast times getting home from Woolwich.

When I came back early one winter night, around eleven, Irma and Eddy were having a quiet drink of cider, so I joined them. Eddie went to bed after a while and I saw my chance. I put another log on the fire, holding Irma in my arms and overcome with something I had never experienced before - passion for a woman. It was mutual lust that neither of us could contain. Tearing at each other's clothes, as the red flames of the fire danced round the room, I found at last a release - opening the gate to my imprisoned sexual psyche that I had contained since childhood. I took Irma to my bed in the next room where we slept till the morning. We were both awakened by Eddie as he went to work.

I didn't know how to react to his behaviour, not saying anything about us being together. I had, I suppose, a pretty dominant personality at the time, full of nervous energy and very outgoing. Finding a new stability in my life, was I perhaps presenting something of power and freedom in their house? Was he finding it hard going with the responsibility of his wife and children? Maybe I had come as a counter to his mundane life, telling of my experiences in the Merchant Navy, Borstal, and prison episodes. Could Irma have been attracted by this freedom I represented? Eddie's mother had come from travelling stock and could curse with well-described inflection, telling us once of her inability to have sex, *"My old mank is shrivelled up tighter than a cow's horn."* I was taken aback by her use of language and lack of embarrassment. I mention this because I had a run-in with her when I took Irma to the local pub where everyone knew them. She accused me of breaking up the family by being with Irma, and said I should clear out. I answered her back by saying it was up to Eddie to sort it out, not her. I was finding it hard staying in the same house as Irma. I was jealous of Eddie sleeping with her, but did not have the guts to do anything about it. I could not be tied down, but craved for her every day, confused about what to do and torn between staying and going.

I decided to have a six weeks trial, going back home to see how things would work out. Irma came to see me during that time, but neither of us spoke about how we were feeling. In the end I more or less gave up thinking about her by going back to work and meeting up with the Woolwich crowd again. I had no interest in crime during those years, doing my best to unravel my psyche and have a decent relationship with women. The alienation was hard to understand, always feeling so introverted compared to my friends who seemed to be having such a good time. Like the expression goes, having a monkey on my back, forever irritating, giving feelings of not belonging.

I had another episode of psychotic madness when I was living with Irma. I went to Woolwich with the school pal who introduced me to the cider house after returning from evening classes. We were drinking in a family social club when my friend poured a full pint of beer over the head of a teenage girl he was talking to. Her brother came across, wanting to start trouble, so I snapped and a fight started between me and the girl's brother: plus some of his friends joined in too. I was beaten about a bit and left in a heap in the alley. I came round and returned to the bar three times before I was eventually knocked unconscious. I finished up in St Nicholas' Hospital, Plumstead again, badly bruised but lucky not to have any broken bones. The secretary of the club came in to see me, begging me not to return for the characters that beat me up. He was most concerned as he didn't want me seeking revenge, knowing how determined I had been last time. It must have been a frightening time for the children, seeing all that violence and blood on my face and clothing. I reassured him I wouldn't return. I had to wear sunglasses in the middle of winter until the black eyes and swollen nose returned to normal, much to the delight of my father to whom it no doubt brought back memories of his own youth.

I got a job at Erith working for Lings, a local building firm, painting the local unmarried mothers' home. I met Shirley there and before the job was finished we were married. I quite understood her fear of having sex before we were married. She had been let down before, so I just had to get wound up with the heavy petting until we were married. Then the worst of scenarios took place: I had such psychological blocks that our marriage was never consummated. I went through hell, getting more and more depressed until she left. I was devastated; I could not think straight. I did stupid things like moving to the place where she had met the father of her child, Paula. I went to Filey, near Scarborough, thinking that just being there might develop into something. Prior to going there I managed to find out which removal van took her things and where. I found the fellow she had gone with and where they were staying. I had no one to share the pain with until I broke down in the kitchen one day, crying on my mother's lap like a six-year-old child, very near to a nervous breakdown. After six months I left Scarborough, having been a 'Spieler' for a showman giving a spiel about a Dracula victim who had lost her body, backed by the music from *The Night on Bear Mountain* and Holst's *'Mars: Bringer of War'*. All this was very effective, alongside the image of a young girl without a neck – all done by mirrors. I frequented illegal bookies, spending my money and deeply depressed amongst the northern holidaymakers enjoying themselves. I was trying hard not to return to crime, breaking into local houses just to get the fare home. Girls never interested me at the time either, as my libido was non-existent. I had opportunities to date one or two of the girls in the show who were lonely, and the landlady's daughter made overtures on a few occasions, but I couldn't get Shirley out of my mind.

I eventually borrowed the money to get back to Erith and started the weekend rounds with the usual Woolwich drinking partners. My mother and Joe went fruit picking in Kent and I became involved with one of my ex-Borstal mates who was setting marcasite stones in eternity rings. I had some from him, which I pledged in all the S.E. London pawnbrokers, getting a third of their value then throwing away the tickets. I ran out of shops after a time and was not too disposed towards going back to decorating, so tried my hand at setting marcasites. I was an utter failure, not having the skill for it. He was continuously pressing me to do a crime with him, as he had inside information from the manager of a company in Shepherds Bush. I eventually gave in when my younger brother was charged with stealing a motorbike and looked like getting imprisonment for the first time. I did the crime and got £1,000 from it, but my so-called friend tricked me out of £250 of the money. This was to play an important part in the events that followed. The crime had nothing to do with safe blowing, so I had no fear of it being associated with my previous convictions - or so I thought.

I got my brother a local solicitor, who managed to get him probation, much to my delight. I then went on a spending spree with Ann, a young girl I met through the schoolmate responsible for my being beaten up at the Social Club. Ann was a friend of his girl Rosie. Both came from the Manor Park area of London. We found a room in a house at Woodpecker Road, New Cross, owned by a Turkish Cypriot couple. In the room next to us were two nurses who worked at New Cross Hospital, one of whom had tremendous legs. I had now lost the depression and got my libido back.

It was wonderful having a normal relationship with Ann, after the agony of my sexual and mental state

164

when married to Shirley. I soon forgot Shirley, settling down to an easy life with this attractive younger woman. I'd put the money in a Post Office account and drew on it every day. I was also mixing with a criminal crowd in Woolwich, who suspected I had done some villainy. It wasn't long before the local informers were getting a breakdown on my background from the law. I became suspicious when I was approached by someone who mentioned my past and said they would like me to blow a safe the next time they did a job. This was stupid, asking me to do this when I was not known to anyone in the area other than the law. I was thus put on my guard, saying nothing about my life but mindful of a warning given by the friend in Wandsworth when I was on remand six years previously. He'd warned me to keep away from Woolwich as it's full of informers.

One night, a fellow I had not seen for many years sorted me out in a pub. He said the safe where he works would be easy and he knew which night it would have money in it. I was by now getting even more suspicious. After this obvious ploy to get me fitted up so I would do the job, only to have the police there waiting to pounce.

I was now enjoying myself with Ann, after years in a wilderness of a kind. I was finding my true self at last, dancing in the pub to the music of Elvis and others of that era. It was 1958: I was in my twenty-sixth year and thinking seriously of settling down with Ann. After a time she became pregnant, so I suggested she could get a termination by a woman I knew - if that was what she wanted. For some reason it didn't work, so she decided to keep it. I had been invited to her parents' home on the Sunday of the thirteenth of April 1958: it was a cold day with some hard-packed snow still left on the side of pavements. On one of the paths I saw her sister's initials written in chalk, saying that so and so loves the initialled person. Ann found this amusing and remarked on it. I was nervous about meeting her parents, not knowing if Ann had told them of her condition. She also had an aunt and uncle there, who came from the Ealing area of London. Her aunt spoke of her work in an unmarried mothers' home.

In the evening we listened to her young sister play Old King Cole on the piano, much to the admiration of the parents. I then went with Ann's father to the local pub, The Governor General. On the way there, we watched the Russian space probe go over at 8.20 p.m. and admired the wonder of such an exploit and the Russian supremacy in space. We spoke about Ann and her friend Rosie, whom he blamed for her influence. He ran his hand through his hair saying, *"She has made me grey, that girl,"* breathing a deep sigh of dejection. I was not forthcoming about any of my own background, but was sympathetic to his plight, thinking *"well she is with me now"*. On returning to the house, we listened to his younger daughter play The Grand Old Duke of York on the piano. We left in good humour, walking to the bus stop near Manor Park Station, and using an alley-way to relieve myself on the way. Before crossing the road towards the bus stop, I commented on a man dressed in bowler hat and striped trousers carrying an umbrella, saying he was early for work in the morning. We got the bus to New Cross, paying the fares to a blonde conductress, a little on the plump side, looking admiringly at Ann's fashionable pink fake fur coat. We arrived at New Cross at twenty past twelve by the clock on the Town Hall.

Ann had to leave on the Tuesday to look after her sister for the rest of the week. On Thursday night I went to the dogs at Charlton with my two brothers. When we arrived back at New Cross, the law came in full handed, making it difficult to move in the room with nine people in there. I fumed at them and cursed. Why were they here? I had nothing to fear, knowing I was clean in all respects to do with crime. After I had calmed down a little, they decided to take me somewhere, giving my two brothers permission to stay there and to tell Ann what had happened to me. I was driven to Scotland Yard where a copper peered at me through the wet window (for it was raining hard) saying, *"All right take him off"*. I later learned that this fellow was a top cop, appointed to break the gangs responsible for safe-blowing cinemas and other places in the Home Counties. He was eventually given some recognition for doing just that, which would include my wrongful conviction.

The journey was like something from Kafka. As we travelled towards the West Country in heavy rain, I had

167

no idea where I was heading or why. They started with crude banter about the size of a copper's dick, to make light of the journey and to get me to loosen up as I was keeping quiet in fear of being 'verballed' - as is their wont. Then the chat turned to a case one of them had been involved with, where a young chap had been charged with breaking and entering. When talking about girls in the town he'd been with, it transpired that he had been with the daughter of a local dignitary and was not aware of her age. They charged him for having sex with a minor, which warranted a stiffer sentence. They all thought this a laugh and then continued with a question to me, that I stupidly commented on by saying, *"I suppose they put you onto me"* (which in common slang terms means 'they gave you my name' - which doesn't mean that I was involved)

I was taken to Guildford Police Station, where a copper was dropped off: a small chap with a pencil moustache looking more like a spiv than a copper. Then on to Aldershot nick where I was put into a cell, still unaware of why I was there. On Friday morning the weather turned for the better, making me angrier at being confined in this bloody place, with Ann frantic not knowing what was happening to me.

I was arraigned before a special court on the following Monday, where the verbal statement was put before the court quoting what I had said, *"I suppose that Mottingham mob put you onto me."* This was true, but taken out of context. On the basis of that verbal I was held in custody until an identity parade was arranged. I still did not know what the charges were or the reason for my court appearance. I was eventually put on an identity parade but, just before I went up to appear on it, a copper came through the door and said, *"Have you been on one before: do you know what to do? You can change places at any time with anyone in the line up".*

I did this as I watched three people walk slowly along the line nine times, three times each. A fourth person then walked along the line another three times. I was by now getting fed up, so I looked at this fellow on his last time past. He then picked me out. I did this because I was getting fed up with the waiting, knowing that I was bloody innocent and had nothing to fear. But this was what the police wanted, for through my ignorance and anger at being made to be there, I did the worst thing I could have done. I looked at the idiot, who had no idea what he was doing. I realised what a fool I had been and when they took me down to the cells again I naturally screamed abuse at them all for putting me in that position. What an experiment it would be to arrange the parades with a subject who looks at the person trying to pick out the criminal? I am aware now that evidence based solely on the identity parade is no longer admissible in court.

I was placated after a few minutes when the police came down in force, ready to subdue me should I lash out at them. I was charged with the cinema offence at Guildford as well as the Aldershot cinema safe breaking. The police were now cock-a-hoop at having a body with a previous record for that type of crime. They were convinced that I was responsible, regardless of what I said. I believe Ann gave a statement to them regarding the night we had been at her mother and father's. I gave a statement which corroborated this. I believe this was given to the police at Manor Park who then called at Ann's house at two in the morning, annoying her father so much that he no longer wanted anything to do with me.

I had to go to the Magistrates Court again to have depositions heard, before a date for trial was fixed for Hampshire Quarter Sessions on the 26th June 1958. It was here that I read a letter sent to a local solicitor which had been left on the desk where a Mr Kennedy was speaking on my behalf. The letter stated that the police were sure Farquhar was responsible for the crimes he is charged with. Did Kennedy leave this open for me to read? I will never know, but when cross-examining the police witness who had picked me out at the parade, a man called Allen Gent, Kennedy asked him if the person he saw at the rear of the cinema, at twelve in the evening, with his girlfriend in a car with windows steamed up, was wearing a hat? And if so was it a cap or trilby? Mr Gent didn't know what he was wearing.

I was now beginning to get a clearer picture of what had happened on the night the two fellows blew the two safes in Guildford and Aldershot. They were seen leaving the cinema at Guildford between twelve and half-past. The taller of them, described as 'very tall' came towards the parked car and peered through the windscreen, trying to see if it was occupied. The distance he was away was never mentioned. The thieves had found little in the safe so had gone to the Cinema at Aldershot, which was a hundred yards from the police station, and had stolen over £900. Their car had been left at the rear with the engine still warm. This was noticed by a patrolling bobby who noted the number plate. The same car was later involved in an accident at Brentford, where the driver, the taller of the two, wrote down an address that proved false. This was given as evidence to a handwriting expert, Dr Nichols, Director, Police Laboratory who stated that my sample given later whilst in Winchester Prison meant I could not have written this.

While I was in Winchester Prison, a solicitor wrote to me saying that Mr Howecroft, Ann's father, would not under any circumstances go to court on my behalf. After an exchange of letters, I realised that the solicitors didn't believe me so I dismissed them. I was given another firm, Shenton, Paine and Brown, a firm based in Basingstoke. After some correspondence with them, I was visited by one who had no idea what to do. I lost my temper with him when he asked what I did when I got out of the car. I replied, *"What fucking car; I am not guilty. I know nothing of the car. I was miles away with an alibi. The fellow who picked me out made a mistake because I looked at him"*. With

171

that he left. I then realised I would be better off defending myself, and only wished I had done so from the beginning, since the whole so-called defence was a farce. The police had got to the solicitors just as they did at the preliminary hearings. Kennedy had left the letter on the table stating they strongly believed me to be guilty. What chance did I have under such circumstances with a Legal Aid defence Counsel?

The Trial – Hampshire Quarter Sessions

My mind no more dwells on painted codes
Ordered to peaceful judgement like a poem'
But in a cold dark vault under court
Where justice is murdered.
And in the cells I see the trampled bodies of the dead
And hear the living shriek; and those who are the most disfigured
I yet recognise as the most just.
Trial of a judge
S. Spender

When I eventually arrived at the court, the Counsel shook my hand saying, *"What have we got here then?"* at the same time offering me a Players cigarette, which I refused, still angry at what he said. I could not believe what I was hearing. What does he mean? Hasn't he been briefed? *"Ann and her mother are here as witnesses, all will be well"* - or so I thought - *"when they are called"*.

Then came the next blow, for, as the prosecuting counsel came through the door, a gasp went up from the court - Inskip, the leading counsel in the county was appearing for the police. The scales of so-called justice had been tipped in favour of the Crown from the beginning, and no doubt the prosecution, the main player in this drama, was higher in legal standing than the Deputy Recorder. He was, I believe, a retired naval man presiding over the trial. Inskip wore a black eye patch, instantly inspiring sympathy from the jury.

The whole morning was taken up with what I can only describe as time wasting - producing my clothes that had been sent to a forensic police laboratory for signs of explosive particles and safe insulation. All my footwear had been inspected and samples had been taken with a cocktail stick from my fingernails. This last detail was not mentioned in court, as it would have added to the negative results that were found against me. After lunch it was the turn of the witnesses who spoke to the two men in the car at Brentford. They said they could not pick out anyone from the identification parade. There were no questions from the so-called barrister, supposedly defending me; about whether it was me they had seen.

Then their main and only witness was called. When asked what he did at the identity parade, he replied, *"I picked out the man who looked most like him."* There was quite naturally some uproar when he said this. The slippery Inskip, realising the mistake, countered by saying *"Can you see the man in court who you picked out at the parade?"* Quite obviously he picked me. This must have placated the jury, as the lies went on and there were no questions again from my defence regarding Gents answer in regard to the hats when the depositions were taken. Then the devious Inskip asked the Recorder if Mr Gent, who leads a busy life as a businessman, would like to be excused to return to his work. There wasn't any request from my counsel for him to stay, which again showed how my defence was working hand in glove with the prosecution. What had happened to the copies of statements taken at the lower court when depositions were taken? I had never seen them, so can presume they had been conveniently lost. The whole trial appeared to have been a process of collusion between the prosecution and the so-called defence, to seek a verdict of guilty [in order to rid the Home Counties of safe crackers]. The authorities wanted results. The police at Aldershot had informed my solicitors that I had previous offences for this type of crime and that they were certain that I had committed these crimes.

When the firm had sent a solicitor to take a statement from me a few days before the trial, he asked me the most stupid questions such as, *"What did you do when you got out of the car?"* He obviously believed the police when asking that type of question. The whole trial was a farce from beginning to end. I was badgered not to go into the box for my own benefit because they had no intention of calling witnesses on my behalf. Ann and her mother were not called. They could have given me a perfect alibi on the night of the crimes.

I made the solicitor promise to appeal on my behalf if it went the other way and I was found guilty. He agreed to that. The police read the report from Dr Nichols, director of the Police Laboratory in Wales, which said that on no account could my handwriting be the same as that of the tall man who gave the false address and name when he had the accident. The Recorder then asked both Counsels to approach the Bench because each blamed the other for not requesting Nichols to attend the court to give evidence. They approached the Bench a few times, arguing points of law and no doubt discussing my previous conviction for the same offence. Perhaps they also discussed the police interest in this case, since Scotland Yard was on record as wanting to see this type of crime stopped at all costs.

A person with my background is looked upon as part of an underclass - *'So what if he goes down!'* When the time came for both Counsels to give their closing speeches to the jury, I had been badgered not to go into the box as they were arguing over the fact that the prosecution had not proven their case. Inskip spoke about the only witness for the Crown's evidence as being damning for me and *"would Mr Gent gild the lily in this case?"* I never had a statement taken from me by the defence solicitor. My witnesses were not called to back my rightful alibi. The police had got to the solicitors, damning me in the letter that Mr Kennedy had perhaps left open deliberately on the table for me to see.

Had I conducted my own defence, or had a retrial, these would have been my main arguments - ineffectual defence because of the police influence on the solicitors. And, of course, the mix up by the police in not bringing the handwriting expert to court as a witness because it would have prejudiced their chance of winning, as well as making the man Gent what he was - a liar. My looking at him was the only reason I was chosen because I was the only one in the line-up to do it. The three other people who came before him quite naturally walked along nine times between them and he had done three so was feeling as though it all relied on him to find someone. I was foolish to look at him.

The jury had been out around an hour or so when they brought in the only verdict they could, that of guilty. It was a forgone conclusion. Police came in from the other courts to hear the outcome and gave a muffled exclamation of satisfaction, as their colleagues had secured a guilty verdict through their devious endeavours, by twisting evidence in their favour. After my previous convictions had been read out by Detective Sergeant Anderson, he went on to explain that the reason explosive particles had not been found on my clothes was that I had worn overalls. How clever they were - making up pieces to fit the puzzle! He then went on to say that I had deposited a thousand pounds in a Post Office bank account. This, of course, was true but it had been some weeks before the crime was committed. He didn't mention that, did he? He then went on to say that I was a young man of high intelligence and the reason they believed I had gone back to crime after six years was over the break-up of my marriage.

I was asked by the Recorder if there was anything I wished to say to the court before he passed sentence –

but I must not allude to anything to do with the proceedings of the day. I had been caught on the hop, so to speak, unprepared for this, but did say something about the court's proceedings being quick and that the verdict was wrong and that I would appeal. I then spoke about something I had heard from my Prison Education Officer during a class at Lewes Prison. He said that, in a play from Shakespeare, two murderers brought before the King were asked, *"Why are you the way you are?"* One replied, *"Because we are made that way sire."* I said, *"I was once like those prisoners, but chose to change my way of life as a criminal because I changed my values in life. But today, as one woman knows, I am completely innocent, and shall appeal."* I then sat down in time to see Inskip's smirk of defiance as he rose from his seat to leave the court, no doubt to celebrate with the police for a good day's work, putting another villain off the streets for three years.

Some weeks later, the solicitor from Shenton, Paine and Brown came to see me as promised, very agitated, asking if I had written anything regarding my appeal. I spoke about what I'd done then he left. I had the papers on my lap ready for him to look at but he said nothing about helping me as arranged at the trial. He couldn't get out fast enough. I felt *"what a bastard, I hope that's not the last I'll see of him"*, but deep down I felt that would be it, and wished I'd had a chance to hit him. Another let-down by the defence who didn't want to do anything on my behalf. I was a stooge, set up by the whole so-called justice system.

I had applied for a 'Leave to Appeal' form from the prison, but I hadn't any idea how to fill it out so I wrote about my alibi, visiting Ann's parents on the night of the crimes, thinking that would be enough. In my ignorance I expected the solicitor to help me. How foolish that belief was, in hindsight, for all it would have done was to expose their ineptitude in defending me. My application for Leave to Appeal was refused.

The morning after my return from the court, I had to go again through the same routine of seeing the Governor, but this time as a convicted prisoner. I was beckoned in by the Principal Officer and asked to give my name and number to the Governor. I did so. Half way through the sentence, as it was being read out to me, I felt overwhelmed by the injustice of my position and said, *"I ain't fucking well going to do it,"* whereupon the three officers protecting the Governor manhandled me out the door. They put me by a door leading to the yard and, on opening it, told a maintenance screw with two inmates to take me to the Mailbag Shop. They knew the procedure for taking out disgruntled idiots like me.

The rest of my time in Winchester Prison was served in the Mailbag Shop, brooding over the events that led me to be sewing stitches eight to the inch, until it was time for my transfer to another prison.

It wasn't long before I was transferred to Wandsworth, for allocation to a suitable prison for the Training. During my interview with a Deputy Governor, he

179

lifted his head from my record and asked the usual question, *"Why are you a criminal?"* Much to his annoyance my reply was, *"I became a criminal because I chose to, just as another boy would choose to be a train driver."* This could not have been the norm, as taught in his criminology classes prior to becoming a governor. We had a few more heated words before he curtly dismissed me. He was still agonising over my reply about choosing to be a crook. On leaving the room I asked for a prison with a good library as a priority. Before leaving Wandsworth I was led to Huxley's *Perennial Philosophy*: at Maidstone I was directed towards other writers. I say 'led' because it came at a time when I was most in need of it. I have read of others who remark on this phenomenon, of books coming their way when they needed help. I believe this to be a form of intervention, I am sure. From my unknown Editor, Angel, or Guide.

MAIDSTONE 1958

It was a wet, dreary day as we left Wandsworth by coach en route to Maidstone prison, the place I had first seen as a young boy. My uncle Ted had been in there doing time and I had been shown it by the son of the foster parents who gave me my first home as an evacuee at the age of seven. There were about seventeen of us on transfer that day, all deep in thought as we headed toward the county town of Kent. There wasn't a word spoken as the coach went on its dreary way, each too wrapped within himself to peer from the windows, as the rain reflected the dejection we all felt as the coach journeyed on.

As we arrived at the reception area we were all completely bowled over by the attitude of the screws, who spoke to us with warmth far removed from what we had been used to back at 'Wanno' [a nickname for the worst nick in the London area]. This was something I had difficulty accepting. We were taken to the dining room – tablecloths … real cutlery … another mystery. Was this the officers' mess? We had a job taking it in but relished the change. Eating food under this new, relaxed atmosphere was pure joy, giving us plenty to talk over during the meal. Sleep came easier that night, anticipating the same changes in the morning that we had experienced in reception.

I recognised old faces from Woolwich during the course of the day, telling me how long they had left to serve and what to expect from the place. Clarke, one of the Cannery Row characters, rubbed it in when he discovered how long I had got. He said how little he had left, laughing as he commiserated with me for my three years. There was Batham, a fellow I had once hit because he knocked his girl about one night in the pub. Spike Lewis gave me the same treatment later. There was also Peter Power, who had a deformed hand, nicknamed Wingy to his pals. I was to be with him on exercise for most of my time, as we were both doing roughly the same time - known in prison parlance as a lagging.

I had an interview with the Housemaster, a fresh-faced, youthful, well-built man who looked like a rugby player in his early forties. He smiled as he lifted his head from my record and asked why I was a criminal. I said, *"I'm not guilty and shouldn't be here, but if you want to know how I became a criminal in the past, then I suppose you could say because of women."* I was thinking of my mother in particular. He gave a broad smile back, without questioning my assertion of innocence, and went on to say the usual official authority mantra, *"look after yourself, keep out of trouble, and we shall get along all right; OK Farquhar"*. His name was B.E.N Lyte.

I was still surprised at how the officers treated us, such a far cry from what I had experienced in the past. I was later to realise that the more freedom you allow, the more you allow that freedom to be abused. Give them an inch and they take a mile, as the saying goes. I saw a lot of this happen here: indeed, on one occasion I felt sorry for an officer, when a prisoner openly argued with him. This would never have happened with the old regime: you didn't say anything or else you would be banged up in the chokey cells. These were my first impressions of Maidstone Prison. All in all, a decent place to be, as nicks went in 1958, but not if you were innocent.

I applied for a form to petition the Home Office as soon as I could, informing the Governor of my situation, of not being guilty. The reply stated that unless I had new evidence not presented at the trial it was a waste of time. Ann's parents would not help me under any circumstances, and Ann was arranging with the local Social Services to have our baby adopted, so I was far from her mind under the conditions she had to bear. She was living by herself in a bed-sit without help from her parents, because of the shame they felt over her getting involved with me and having a baby. I wanted nothing more than to be with Ann and the child: I had taken her to an abortionist only because that had been her decision. This all added to the heartbreak and dejection I felt as a consequence of the court's verdict. I had already had eighteen years of depression since being evacuated at eight and returning home to find my mother living as one of the local whores of the town and living in nothing more than a brothel. Being with

Ann was the best thing that had happened to me since meeting Shirley. Finding a sexual partner after having the problems associated with my sexual sublimation over the years was something I didn't want to lose under any circumstances.

Irma was the first to break through my relationship problems (those due to my sexual suppression), but even then it only partially helped. I was still not fully free from the mindset of my criminal background, like borrowing motorbikes to get home when I was drunk.

Having to do time for something you didn't do is the hardest of punishments because there's a feeling of not belonging to the prison structure: it's as if you are there just for the visit and somehow there's a possibility that you will get out. I could not accept that I was part of the regime. When I went down to the cells at Hampshire Quarter Sessions after being sentenced, I began to sing to cheer myself up, aware at last of the truth and the puny evidence the Crown had. In my naivety, I felt elated. It would all come out in the wash: I had been buoyed up by the promise of help from the solicitor, confident when the appeal was heard that it would be home again to help Ann.

Later on in Winchester, it became apparent that I was getting nowhere and the odds were stacked against me. I began to lose confidence and went through feelings of insecurity. For instance, I could only sleep on the floor of the cell, not even on the lowest bunk, which was only six inches high. I began to dream of release, then wake up to the horror of the sentence. Fortunately I had my own cell in Maidstone, but the nightmares didn't cease. I got persistent stomach trouble at all hours, without much to ease it other than bismuth, which never worked. I began to feel weak, knowing that if a rope were thrown over the wall I would not have had the strength to climb out. Once in the shower I was whistling away, when another fellow asked me to stop it as he had a headache. Because of my weakness I had to stop for him: I didn't have the strength to confront him. In the past I would have said to him, *"Yes I'll stop for you, if you'll do the same for me"* then see how he answered that. This time I couldn't do anything about it.

I was reading a lot, petitioning every six weeks, getting the same reply. Some months later I was threatened for breaking the rules with my persistent petitioning *"which was not consistent with good order and discipline in the prison." The* Governor's name was Ffinch. He was a religious man and a fair one, allowing me to carry on with the petitions. I was aware that his predecessor, a reforming Governor called Vidler, was personally responsible for the way the prison was run. It was rumoured he'd choose the prisoners he wanted for Maidstone from the dispersal prisons in London. Ffinch no doubt carried on with the reforming changes, with the help of the Home Office.

I was eventually given a six months' training course in basic *'Fitting'* that helped to keep my mind occupied - filing bits of metal, learning how to use a micrometer and a vernier gauge. During the evenings I went to as many classes I was allowed - Stained Glass, Current Affairs and the Music Appreciation on Saturday afternoons. This was mainly attended by the gay contingent, some of whom were later caught having it off under the stage. I enjoyed the music classes: in those days it was the only chance to hear music of any description. The tutor running the Current Affairs class was a man named Len Powell. Len met me for a cup of tea in the ABC restaurant the day I left Maidstone: he also became my Prison Visitor and lifelong friend for more than thirty years.

Sometime during the course, I found a copy of The Middle Way: the Buddhist Journal with contributions by the late Christmas Humphreys. He was the prosecuting counsel responsible for sending Ruth Ellis to the gallows; the last woman to be hanged in this country. He said Karma was responsible for the outcome. The Buddhist doctrine of non-attachment attracted me as I read the Journal and the articles of Dr Suzuki in particular. Such abstract observation from one of his sayings … the tea ceremony is compatible with the creation of the Universe. I read the Bhagavad-Gita after having read Kenneth Walker's autobiography, *'I Talk of Dreams'*, wherein it's mentioned. Such were my stepping-stones to books along the way. I read other works by Walker, and Victor Gollancz's *'From Darkness To Light'*, an anthology of powerful spiritual observations.

I felt I was once again led, this time to a copy of the Sunday Express that had been discarded in the waste bin. As I read an article on 'Unitarianism' I soon realised that I was thinking along the same lines. I had had trouble with the belief that Jesus was the only Son of God, and I believed that the resurrection was a myth. I decided I wanted to change my religion and become a Unitarian. It was founded out of the anger of not being guilty yet bodily imprisoned, though my mind could not be imprisoned. I made the request to change my religion and was given three white sheets of yellow-edged A4 paper with various questions such as *"why do you want to change your religion?" "Which religion do you want to change to?" "Why do you want to change to that particular new religion?"*

I duly filled them in, noticing they carried some sort of official paper numbers. I was told they represented documents printed in 1914. I had more or less forgotten about them when, six or more weeks later, I was asked by an officer to go with him to the gate, as I had a woman visitor.

In prison the smallest of situations is magnified into a major event. It's the limited world you live in. I immediately assumed that, being a woman, she would have some news about my wrongful imprisonment and was there to help me get my freedom. Having a visitor at the gate compounded the thoughts, because it's very rare that you get visits at the gatehouse. When I saw the person, my heart sank. Who was this middle-aged woman in a tweed costume with her hair done in a bun like a school Headmistress?

After the initial shock and disappointment I began to warm toward her quiet manner and beautiful voice. She said her name was Muriel Hilton and that she was the lay preacher at Maidstone Unitarian Church. *"I'm pleased to meet you, Mr Farquhar."* It all clicked into place as I shook her hand. Then, sitting down together, we talked for two hours, referring to Huxley, Walker, and other aspects of how I felt about Christianity and my new-found interest in Buddhism. My experience with Muriel led to a lifelong friendship. Some months later she wrote of it as a 'timeless moment' in an article for the Unitarian newsletter *'The Enquirer'*. What I gained from that meeting was the recognition that someone had accepted me without judgement. I was a young man trying to make changes in his spiritual life after having been put down by authoritarian structures, courts, schools, army, and prisons. Muriel encouraged my search for knowledge, giving me a feeling of worth as a human being. She did not see me as a criminal.

The Education Officer in Lewes prison saw me in the same light - as a young man worthy of help. Muriel spoke about authors she thought I would like to read and offered to send them to me. I found John Stewart

Collis particularly interesting, and even now I still have some of his books. Muriel was a personal friend and told him about me. I have a letter where he says he would find prison conducive to his own study and writing. I was also inspired by the works of John Cowper Powys.

To complete my application for change of religion I had to have an interview with the Prison Chaplin. He asked why I wanted to become a Unitarian, and whether I realised that it was a very small group in comparison to the Church of England. *"How can you belong to such a group, when the whole of Protestant England is right?"* The article had mentioned that there were only forty thousand Unitarians at that time. He made it very clear that he didn't like my leaving the flock, and dismissed me, saying that I was heading for the deepest and darkest of depths. Before I closed the door, I said I had never felt more enlightened.

I applied to see the Visiting Magistrates, to tell them of my plight, in the hope that something could be done: but it was a waste of time. I spoke my piece about the fact I had been somewhere else on the night of the crimes, but was not impressed by the stance they all took while listening to my case. I was later told there was nothing they could do, so I applied to see the Visiting Committee, another body of volunteers willing to listen to those with a grievance in prison. They could all have been clones of the

Magistrates: a grey-haired, po-faced, ineffectual body of people who just listened as I ranted on about why I shouldn't be in the prison. Again another knock back, as it's called in prison parlance, so what next?

The fitters' course lasted six months, and during that time the prison started a magazine that I thought was a good idea. I was friendly with the fellow who surprised me by taking on the role of editor. I contributed to the first edition by writing an article headed *'On the Serious Side'*, a piece about the nuclear threat and my contention that having the knowledge to make it would not in any way help toward non-proliferation. I pride myself on using the phrase before Khrushchev, describing it as being above us like the *'Sword Of Damocles.'*

I was now part of the works party, erecting scaffolding and painting officers' houses outside the prison. I could have walked off at any time during the day. Imagine my presence of mind, doing a sentence for a crime I hadn't committed then being put on trust each day not to abscond!

I had visits from Muriel and was allowed to walk with her in the flower garden within the prison. This was, to my mind, the first time a woman had ever been allowed to do this. I felt proud being with her on those occasions, talking of books and my life in the prison. I never spoke to Len or Muriel about my innocence.

One of the joys of being amongst men is that somewhere within a group there will be a clown: I was privileged to have been with such a group. His name was James and time in prison with him was non-existent. I owe my sanity to this man, for his ability to take the smallest of situations into side-splitting cameos of genius in the making. James came from Weston Super Mare. It was rumoured he had fallen out with a long-term friend and harmed himself with a shard of broken glass from his cell window. His lampoon of an American Marine, pinned down on a beach under enemy fire, calling for stretcher bearers and then lighting a cigarette for a wounded buddy just had to be seen. The exact way in which his imaginary hat tipped to the back of his head was brilliant. I hope, James that you have had a good life: you deserved it for the pleasure you gave the painting team.

Shirley came to see me about a divorce, which I refused out of anger for the way she treated me. Had I any sense, I should have asked her for money and used it to obtain transcripts of the trial, but I seemed to be in a state of funk about anything concerning an appeal. She was in a position to give me the money to get things rolling, whereas neither my father nor mother could afford to. I wrote to my MP at Erith, Norman Dodds, and so did my father, but nothing could come of this until all the legal avenues had been exhausted.

As far as getting anything done about my case was concerned, I had run out of options, and was now left with my last chance of help - speaking to the Chaplin, the man who said I was heading for the darkest of depths in my spiritual quest. He came to my cell one dreary, wet Sunday afternoon, and when I asked if he could help me, he abruptly answered *"No!"* at which point he hurriedly left the cell, locking it with his own keys. At that point I lost all hope of redress and broke down, calling for God to help me. With my head in my hands I cried out in despair. I had come to the lowest point of my life and could see no way out: I had lost all hope. After years of fighting (one way and another) whatever life threw at me, from evacuation, the air-raids, my mother's actions, her attempted suicide and her near murder of us all, I was now mentally crushed, the culmination of eighteen years' psychological abuse since the age of eight.

I slept better that night than I had for a long time. In the morning I awoke to a bright light across my consciousness which lasted for a few seconds, followed by a feeling of love for all mankind - in particular the police and Gent, the man who had lied all the time, the man responsible for my conviction and for the legal breakdown that occurred. I understood everything, knowing it was all they could do in the mindset they were in. I experienced unity with all life and lost fear of death, because the vision of light left me all-knowing. I had glimpsed behind the curtain, seen what lies behind our limited awareness (which I could only describe as God), with love being the power that enveloped me. I didn't know how to react to this experience but I no longer worried about my sentence. I had forgiven my mother's actions, losing the hate and anger I held against her all my life.

The feeling of love gradually diminished over a period of eight to ten days, lessening a little each day. I was left with a strong sympathy for the underdog, in particular those who were bullied.

The following is an example. One morning we were kept in the prison for some reason or other. While we were standing in groups waiting to return to work, one of the officers who couldn't control the group picked on a friend of mine who was close at hand and smiling. I realised that a wrong had occurred and went off in front of the whole wing, returning to my cell and slamming the door in anger as hard as I could. My friend's name was Forestall and the officer a Mr Scargill. The officer told lies to the Governor when I was on report the following day, saying that he had told Forestall not to misbehave on previous occasions during the lunch periods. It was confirmed that both Forestall and I were working on the outside works party and were never in the prison except for the day in question. I got seven days confined to my cell with a restricted diet. My friend's charges were dismissed and Scargill had a blemish on his record for blatantly lying: no doubt that affected his chances of promotion.

I cannot remember at exactly what stage of my sentence this took place, but I do know that things took a turn for the better. I was made a Blue Band trustee, allowing me to do small things within the prison, such as collecting materials for our work or taking other prisoners to various parts of the prison, thus allowing an officer to do more important things. Later I was given other work in the builders' team, making a new Young Offenders Detention Centre near Ashford Kent. This of course required a return journey daily with the opportunity to see the fair damsels of Kent, the countryside, and wildlife in the grounds of the incipient Centre. My life took on a completely new aspect - being in the prison only rarely was like living in a hostel for the rest of my time. I became stronger, put on weight and above all slept well without nightmares.

During my worst times, prior to my Mystical experience, I found that reading about explorers like Shackleton helped me: sitting on my bed in the warmth of a cell, far removed from the privations they had to endure. Reading about Caryl Chessman's account on Death Row also helped me to see how well off I was. I compared my lot to the situations some have to endure: things such as Iron Lungs and the constant pain a friend of mine suffered. They put it all in perspective. Victor Frankl said that those in the camps who perished first were the prisoners that had difficulties in childhood, not able to see a future of any substance to look forward to. Frankl talks of being given mind-breaking exercises by the guards - like filling a wheelbarrow with earth then having to tip it out and refill it again with the same earth, after wheeling it a long distance, time after time. He tells how he relived memories of his happy childhood to get him through and of the future, when he lectured on his own field of Psychology in Vienna.

As I was nearing the end of the two years, I was put into a pre–release dormitory holding seventeen men. One night I was asked to move my bed away from the window, as some were planning to go out through it. A wet towel was produced then tied around two of the iron bars on the grill; then a chair leg inserted between the towels, acting as a tourniquet. This was then twisted until the bars bent enough for the men to squeeze through. The chaps arranging this were the Scots group who, like all of us in the dormitory, were due for release. I couldn't see the sense in it so, when I was asked if I wanted go with them, I naturally declined.

The rest of the escape plan seemed to go as if scripted for the Three Stooges or some other lunatic gang of miscreants. We wondered what would happen next to the six who had decided to make their way from the dormitory. We watched from four or five windows overlooking the perimeter wall, as the six had somehow made it to the ground and were hurriedly walking around the wall to freedom, stopping every now and then to throw a long white thick rope with a hook of some description over the wall. Unfortunately it didn't catch or hold and fell back down to the eagerly waiting daredevils below. This went on for some time until they went out of sight, only to reappear half hour later, still going through the same routine. They had our sympathy, of course, watching the lads make fools of the system by escaping, but it did have overtones of Burns's poetic observation that "The best laid schemes o' mice an' men gang aft a-gley". They made it eventually, but the governor did not appreciate it. He gave his fatherly homily about the bad publicity given out by the escapes; about what they did to the reputation of the prison and its stature as such a good place to do your time. He was more put out by the fact they stole the rope from the church bell tower than by the escape itself.

I left Maidstone on August the Eighteenth 1960. I had said my farewells to one or two of the notable villains in both the houses (Medway and Kent). One of them, Charlie Wilson, later became one of the Great Train Robbers. My friend and prison visitor, Len Powell, took some papers that I had been putting together as a study of my spiritual growth. We had a drink of tea at Lyon's in Maidstone at half eight in the morning. It was good to do this in recognition of our friendship. Maidstone Prison had become the most important part of my life, in my journey of spiritual growth and meeting my two most guiding influences in Len and Muriel. Was it Karma that caused me to be sentenced for something I hadn't done? Was it a form of poetic justice: making up for that which I had done? Was my experience at seventeen my reward for saving the life of that man (for I had heard a voice saying that I would be rewarded)? Why did I take notice again when this same voice said *"look at him"* when I was standing in the identity parade, getting agitated because of the waiting?

Was this my hidden editor, which I have alluded to over these pages during the course of my life? Or was it perhaps a Guardian Angel leading me to the highest level of consciousness that man can experience?

I believe it was the latter.

Return to Erith 1960

My life has been not so much about living to learn, but rather learning how to live.

I came back to Erith, glad to have put the prison behind me, with much to think about - like work, money and future. Bob was released from another prison the same week and we both obtained work in a factory called Mallensons, a wood laminating company in Thames Road, Crayford. During the course of the two weeks working there, irony of ironies, we spent some time stacking doors which were destined for a prison in Africa. After the customary two weeks' work with one in hand, we had our first wage packet, so we could go out for the first time, after a fortnight at home doing little else than watch television. We wore our clean-pressed suits: glad at last to feel free of work clothing and smart enough for a night to the local flicks at Bexleyheath. If we were lucky we might perhaps chat up some girls, for my brother Bob was now twenty two and we were both looking and feeling good for our first night out.

It was a bright August evening. I was impatient to get to the cinema and getting quite frustrated waiting for the bus. It was a long time coming and an old lady joined us at the stop. At last it came and, as I put my foot on the platform, another came beside mine, covered in a cheap blue canvas shoe. My first thought was, *"why's this cheap-shoed fellow trying to beat me on the bus?"* Then the owner grabbed my arm saying, *"Come on Ron"* and began to pull me off. I remonstrated with him, at the same time pleading with the old lady to see what he was doing to me, hoping for a witness to this idiot's action. She gave me a blank stare and quickly disappeared inside the bus. Who the bloody hell was he, I thought, as I tried to free myself. He said he was a policeman, as another one came from nowhere and grabbed my other arm. I shouted for them to let me go and swung my head to my left hitting the first chap in the mouth. I would have had to be a saint not to retaliate, after serving three years for a crime I had not committed, followed by these two idiots doing what they did. I went hysterical, shouting at them to leave me be and to take their hands off me - which they did. The one I hit with my head had blood coming from his mouth and was trying to stop it with his handkerchief. They took us both to the police phone box nearby and called for a Black Maria and help.

The outcome of that episode was that we were both given two months for assaulting the police, even though my brother did nothing. They lied in court, saying they had told us they were police officers before taking us off the bus and that they wanted to speak to us about my brother John, who was wanted for a crime in London. Later in court I read a letter Bob had sent me, prior to leaving Maidstone, where he stated he would not be going back to Erith for long because of the fear of police harassment. The clerk of the court then countered, saying to the senior copper giving evidence, "This sounds like a very serious attack on your officers, Mr Holland." Mr Holland, being the senior copper at Erith and well known to the court at Dartford, was another member of the Old Boys' club who can do no wrong when conspiring with the court to put away the underclass.

I am reminded of Clarence Darrow's words: "Who will prosecute the prosecution?"

The copper involved in the bus incident then stood up to say his tooth was still loose and that he might lose it.

So after two weeks in the comfort of home, with good cooking, it was back to Wanno for two months, with a third off for good behaviour. I was concerned how Muriel and Len would take my quick return to prison. Had they known the truth about my time in Maidstone being a stitch up by the police and solicitors, they would have understood the reason for my action. I later heard from Len, who said that when Muriel was told she replied, "Yes, Ron is quite high spirited", no doubt alluding to the episode in Maidstone over the Scargill and Forestall affair. My brother Bob was in a worse situation than me, for he had nothing to do with the whole shoddy business, poor chap.

The time went quick enough: I was glad to have only got two months. They could have given me more, had it not been for the letter my brother wrote; of that I'm sure. I eventually visited Maidstone Unitarians for a Service given by Muriel. It was an occasion I'd been looking forward to since first meeting her, pleased to be welcomed by the congregation which included a Mr Omah who, I remember, made me particularly welcome with his broad smile and sure handshake. I was glad to meet them all - Len, Monica, and a Mr Chaney I believe, but still nervous and shy doing so. I was painfully aware of my criminal past, but was helped by the mystical experience which gave me the courage to do it. After reading a little Plato, where he gives a discourse on what is 'Good', I penned the following:

The good is that which makes me see
The inner light that shines in me
That inner light I define the soul
Through introspection makes me whole
For how I love the joys of spring
To hear a Lark sing on the wing
To watch a field of corn wave gently to the wind
This is the good, the inner light
My armour strong that shines so bright
My inner light.

The change from anger, violence, and crime expressed throughout my life, and my inability to have a proper sexual relationship, was now beginning to heal. The words above are proof enough, when compared with others I had written in answer to Wordsworth's famous lines, when I first arrived at Maidstone. [There was a time when meadow field and stream and all the common things in life did seem apparelled in celestial light].

My rider went....*Then all was black, when wind, clouds, and rain with all these elements, did make, a mantel o'er my brow.*

Was I now reaching deeper into my subconscious, allowing the freedom of expression? I think so. Those numinous episodes I experienced in early childhood: hearing school children singing "All things Bright and Beautiful"; seeing the Hedge Sparrow's Nest; when evacuated, visiting the cottage and orchard; watching the Stag in the heather; then, at the age of eleven, writing of the *Mystic Stillness of Water*. These all were signs of my sensitivity, which I had suppressed until encouraged by friendships with Muriel, Len, and the Education tutor at Lewes Young Offenders' Prison as well as my experience in Maidstone. Mr Powell had the same surname as Len in Maidstone, though it was many years before I would speak of the experience in Maidstone to anyone.

I discovered the Unitarian Meeting House in Lewisham, so journeyed there one Sunday to hear the Minister, Jeremy Goring, give an address on the reforming ex-Governor of Maidstone, Mr Vidler. I was naturally surprised at the coincidence, but was once again far too shy, with guilt about my past, to mention to either the Minister, or any of the congregation after the service, about my release from the prison.

I was still living at Erith with my mother and Joe. My mother had settled with Joe, having found a chap who suited her at last. He was eleven years younger than she, but knew how to make money, so they were a good match. I found work in the Woolwich area with other painters I knew and still had the usual weekend drinking sessions – at least for a time. I also sold cheap jewellery as a street trader. I had one of the arch- informers carrying my gear for me: I was pretty sure he was paid by the law to keep a watch on me and report my contacts. I did that for six or nine months in all, before going to the Isle of Wight the following summer to work as a waiter. I made up my mind to leave Erith and Woolwich, after seeing a racial attack on a tall black man in his twenties by a gang of drunken yobs along the Plumstead Road. The whole thing sickened me and made me think this was not what I wanted. They were incensed by some rumour of this fellow's alleged behaviour and went on a kind of rampage, breaking off pieces of fencing to use as weapons with which to beat him. It had finished by the time I got there, but it made me think about what could have happened. He was one of the few black men in the area at the time.

Marriage and Knowing Myself

We stumble and fall, where we might walk with ease.
Change terrifies, especially when change threatens the structure of our
Personal security, so laboriously erected.

Ralph Waldo Emerson.

I went to the Isle of Wight in the summer of 1961, working as a waiter. I enjoyed the freedom, relaxing with plenty of sunbathing, but still found the opposite sex a problem, knowing little if anything of social niceties. But I did learn how to jive. My dancing partner was an attractive blonde waitress from the restaurant where I worked. Like me, she had come to the island for a working holiday. There were good Traditional Bands from London, such as Chris Barber and Ken Colyer, so I was dancing at every opportunity with my new found skill. The Colleges were responsible for a new fad at the time called Skip–Jive that was popular. I was now making up for my lost teen years and the time spent in Maidstone: clearing barriers that prevented my social inclusion, but still a long way to go.

I only saw aesthetic beauty in a woman: the body was still to be discovered. Although on one occasion, seeing my dancing partner place her leg on a stair then swing round showing firm calves and thighs through a tight skirt, I was moved further in my appreciation of the female form. It was a moment akin to the time with the young blonde girl wearing the tight-fitting, grey crepe dress when I had been waiting to enter the dance hall at Erith at the age of fourteen. It was soon after this that I had decided to embark on a life of crime. I felt this re-awakening as a sign of the criminal years starting to mellow at last and something of my true self emerging from the protective shell I had formed as a villain.

I was in digs in Shanklin and a dark-haired, attractive teenage girl lodged in a room next to mine. She frequented the local bookmakers where I attempted a few times to talk to her, but I could never get a suitable response to my ineffectual advances. She told me she already had a boyfriend with a motorcycle, who could take her anywhere. I found the occasional lonely girl on holiday looking for company but that was all.

One day, as I was sunbathing with two of the hotel guests, I saw a tall, good-looking woman sitting close by with a young boy and her mother. The following day she was there with just the boy, and they were sitting closer to our group. I made some overtures to get her attention. The next day she joined us. I enjoyed playing with the little fellow, Kevin, who was eighteen months old - he found the water frightening when the waves came too close. At the end of the day I loaned her my radio for the night and arranged to meet up somewhere. During the course of her holiday we began to spend more time together and I decided to return with her and Kevin when her holiday was over. Her mother had only had the one week so had returned earlier.

I came back to Erith again, this time feeling elated that I had found such a beauty, giving my life some meaning at last. Her name was Greta, after Garbo the actress, and she lived with her brother Tony in flats near the Old Kent Road in South London. Both parents were Catholics: her father was white-haired, caused through his experiences as a soldier in the First World War. He worked as a bus conductor and his hobby was clock and watch repairs: he was well read and particularly acquainted with the works of Dickens.

My life was to take on a new dimension, having another person to share time with. Unfortunately, her father didn't think I was good enough for her: I was, after all, a Unitarian, who didn't believe in the Trinity - and was a common housepainter to boot.

I had found what I had been looking for at last - a woman with a child I could care for. I had such a feeling of pride and compassion for them both, especially when seeing them waving goodbye to me from the flat window when I left. I now had substance to my life and was determined to make it work.

We began to see and learn more of each other over the following months. Greta came to Erith to meet my mother and Joe. We had few friends, so were together most of the time. I had Jim Thorne from Woolwich, of course, and Greta had Joan and Jim Redgwell, who ran a Boxing Club for young lads. Greta worked for The London Electricity Board, as it was then known, and wrote me amusing letters in her spare time. Being a single mother in those days was quite a stigma on your character. I, of course, could not escape the guilt I felt for my past crimes so, in a way, we were attracted by our feelings of alienation.

I told Greta a little of my past. It didn't seem to bother her, other than the fact that I had been self-employed most of my life and hadn't paid any insurance stamps. She mentioned this a few times, asking how we were going to manage in later life without a pension. I found this a rather small problem and retorted that she should have advertised in *'The Times'* for someone with a full set of cards. [*They were all paid eventually.*]

One day, when she was visiting my house, I asked her to fry some potatoes. She replied quite sharply, *"Where's the fat?"* which reminded me of John Wayne, the cowboy, ordering the villain outside for a fight. She showed her feisty individuality on that occasion all right, not prepared for the request - it was then I learnt she couldn't cook. The spuds where swimming in fat. I liked her aggressive attitude though.

We did a lot of our courting walking through the Oxleas Woods, at the top of Shooters Hill, where we watched rabbits, much to Greta's delight: she referred to them as bunnies which amused me for her simple childish nature. We liked going to the 'West End' to savour hot salt beef sandwiches from a bar near the Windmill Theatre, before visiting a cinema. Then perhaps to the White Bear Inn, a gay bar, just to watch the varying types as we sampled our cocktails. Another haunt was the Old Father Thames pub, south of the river, where we would sit and talk in a secluded corner of the near-empty pub. Greta said she was always a wallflower when it came to dancing, being conscious of her height, and consequently made few friends. She was twenty- three by now: six years younger than me.

They were heady days that we shared together, before we married on the 5th of October, 1962 at the Camberwell Registry Office. It was back to Greta's home for a little to eat, and then off to Havant for a few days' honeymoon staying with distant friends of Greta's. Unfortunately Greta's father was not at the Registry Office. It was a very low key affair with the two Jims and Joyce, Jim Thorne's wife. Greta's father stayed in the bedroom away from us all: the only upsetting part of the day. We had a telegram from the congregation at Maidstone, which was a very welcome thought from them. My mother and Joe were unable to make it either.

When we returned to London we took two rooms in Wilcox Road, Lambeth. Kevin stayed with Greta's parents until we settled in and bought furniture. Oonagh was born in our flat on a divan, with Greta facing the window, legs apart, forcing the delivery just as the window cleaner's ladder appeared on the sill. I managed to close the curtains in the nick of time. What a shock it would have been for him if he had looked into the room!

It was the 13th of April, 1963, the same day of the year that I was supposed to have robbed the cinemas in Aldershot and Guildford. I have always taken this to be a sign from a higher power *[A common phrase used today is that coincidences are God's way of remaining anonymous]*. All such events in my life are yet further examples of a gift given by my Guide or Angel. On the 15th of March the following year, 1964, James was born in the local Hospital, 19 inches long and looking like a skinned rabbit with plenty of black hair. Greta hung on until her favourite programme finished - it was called Braden's Beat, a television weekly compered by Bernard Braden, a Canadian broadcaster with a high viewing rating. She went down the stairs smoking a cigarette, glad to enter the ambulance, and delivered James twenty minutes later.

I was selling jewellery from a wooden box shaped like a suitcase, buying plastic beads from a wholesaler in Berwick Street, in London's West End, and selling them in high streets in the provinces, then later in various markets around the country. I would go by Green Line buses during the week, as they were cheaper and quicker in those days.

In the early part of our marriage we went through a bad time. This was, I must confess, due to my feelings of rejection, caused by Greta's actions that I found difficult to handle. I never spoke to her about these feelings, but reacted by brooding over them. I went into a deep pit of anger which I found hard to break from. I began to blame Greta for so many things and lost my temper over the smallest of slights. Greta made friends when she visited the local park with the children, and through one of them was given the address of a house in Lewisham. We later moved there after I paid key money. It was only a small house, but far better than the flat as it had a garden backing onto waste ground which was a hunting ground for Tawny Owls. A little walk further on led to an area where the kids found newts and tadpoles in the spring.

I did a lot of work on the house prior to moving in, as it was in a bit of a state. There was a shop next door, and Lewisham High Street was only a short walk away, with the Unitarian Meeting House no more than a mile. I was far too busy to go to the Meeting House in those days, though I would often see Jeremy Goring, the Minister, driving his mini-bus. He would later become Head, or the equivalent, of a department in Goldsmiths College in New Cross. We were happier there, with good schools nearby and places for the kids to play, including a variety of parks, as well as what at the time were two quiet streets - Nightingale Grove and Knowles Hill Crescent. Muriel commented on the enchanting name of the Grove when responding to my first letter. It was here that I had my second life breakthrough, doing voluntary work for Lewisham Social Services. I was now working in two London markets as a casual stallholder and one in Dartford Kent. I had also learnt to drive by now, so my takings had grown accordingly and I was making my own stretch covers for furniture and caravans: a form of cottage industry that kept me busy. I was managing on three markets quite easily, with no ambition to expand as we had such a comfortable living.

One day, a woman shop owner in East Street Market, Walworth asked how I had done that day. The following week she asked the same thing … and again the following week. I always gave the same answer, *"Not too bad thank you."* I then realised she only wanted to know how much money I had taken.

In the notices one Sunday was an invitation for volunteers under a body called VAL - Voluntary Action Lewisham. I went to the introductory meeting led by Josephine Smith and was accepted to work in a mental health structured group. I did a variety of jobs, from taking a ninety year-old lady home from a hospital ward to collect her nightdress, to taking a partially-sighted pensioner for a ride each Tuesday afternoon to help him cope with the depression he was suffering.

Over a period of three years, Bill and I formed a close bond. He was a small man who was said to have been the first to have a triple heart bypass. He had also been an amateur jockey, among many other things, and had been educated at Felsted Public School in Essex. He later married a showgirl he had met during the First World War when touring with a troupe. He came out a captain after the war, aged twenty-one, and then went up to Cambridge to study agriculture. Subsequently he became Farm Manager for Lady Susan Townley and General Mullins. I took Bill out for a regular run in my Kombi Bus every Tuesday afternoon to various Garden Centres and Nurseries or any other place he fancied. He eventually found his brother, a linguist for Unilever's, and a sister who lived in Ilfracombe, Devon. Bill died just before Christmas 1975 after a spate of bad luck where he lost his friend and Priest, killed on a zebra crossing in the Old Kent Road. His budgie had died the same week, causing Bill to more or less give up.

He was once jostled by a crowd of teenage schoolboys in Sydenham: they ridiculed him and called him a silly old sod. He broke down, sobbing, in the street. He was also very badly treated by the staff in a home for the elderly in Ladywell Lodge, Lewisham.

We had another two girls after Oonagh and James - Donna and Leah. I then had a vasectomy operation in Lewisham Hospital which didn't work out right. My testicle expanded to the size of a grapefruit through a mistake: it was early days for this operation then. It didn't help with my sex life, which became worse after the operation, with Greta more distant and I like a walking time bomb, frustrated more than ever and snapping for the slightest of reasons.

We bought a larger house in Lewisham in 1997, with a drive where I could park my van. I was attending the Unitarians on the odd occasion and was invited by one of the more adventurous members to partake in an 'Encounter Group'. When I learnt what it would entail, I recoiled at the thought of the self exposure. I declined, giving some pathetic excuse, glad to have avoided it. A year later, when working in Woolwich market, I went into Boots the Chemist and picked up a flier on mental health. I had second thoughts about my attitude to change when I read that a normal person should be able to hold a conversation within a group of people. I knew I couldn't do this: I just blushed and stammered, speaking far too quickly and feeling embarrassed after puny attempts to say anything worthwhile.

I decided to do something about it and bought a Time Out Magazine for the first time. Looking under *Groups*, I saw one for Thursday night at Kentish Town, London, so booked up with the leader, a Polish American, named Joe Weslowski. I was looking forward to the prospect of breaking new ground, taking risks of another kind. There were five of us there, all men. Joe did a few bodily exercises initially, and then got us to lie on the floor to get in touch with our emotions, pain and so on. One fellow, Günter, an Austrian who had been a concentration camp guard during the war, was in a bad way: very depressed, saying very little about himself other than the severity of his mental state. I was asked to do a couple of stretching exercises, then to rise as Lazarus from the dead with Joe leaning over me, trying to invoke some form of spiritual presence or energy to raise me from the floor. I hadn't any idea what to do, or where to go if I got up, so stayed down, peering through a half closed eye looking for a door, wondering what I had got myself into with this weird American fellow. After the session I was asked to attend the following Saturday for a full-day workshop. I arranged for Oonagh my daughter to do the market for me at Woolwich that day.

It was a ground breaking experience for me, sharing some of my life in this Encounter Group of a kind, based on the work of Wilhelm Reich, the founder of Bioenergetics, who teaches that the body retains blockages, poor posture and so on, caused by emotional and traumatic experiences, which prevent full expression of natural joy and vigour. We did various body-releasing exercises, like punching pillows, dancing, group embracing techniques and group supporting activities, which I found fascinating and at times quite confronting. I was now hooked on the new awareness I had experienced. Later, I did a variety of groups, seeing the whole Personal Growth movement more as living theatre where we were likened to actors going through our blocked and damaged histories. Not the narcissism some observed it to be. I joined the Humanistic Psychology organisation and received their Journal, 'Self and Society', choosing any group that looked interesting, Primal Therapy, Gestalt, Re-birthing, Co-Counselling, Psychodrama, and another which was a mixture of Rajneesh thinking and 'Est.'. Est. was meant to be expressed in lower case for some reason or other given by the founder, Werner Erhard, an American of Jewish background who introduced 'The Training', as it was known in this country, back in the 80s. I was doing an Adult Evening Class on 'Relationships' with Lewisham Education Department run by a Psychologist who introduced us to the work of Harvey Jackins, the founder of Co-Counselling. He recommended us to do the 'Est.' training after he himself found it beneficial to his life.

I consider the EST Training to have been the fifth most powerful experience in my life. The first was my birth into the world, the second having the experience in Maidstone, the third the family love up to the age of eight when I was evacuated, the fourth having a family of my own with all that it involves, including falling in love with another person, and the fifth 'The Training'. I had to have two goes, before gaining anything from it - being no doubt, such a hard case for treatment. My first training was the second one given in this country and the leader was Charlene Avrenou, an American ex-Weight Watchers counsellor. I found the whole thing mind-blowing and powerful.

What's it like to be in a room with three hundred and fifty other trainees, each wondering the outcome of this so called life changing experience? I was to some degree helped by my earlier group work, and I could by now at least share some of my feelings, but not of this size. I stood to say I had problems in the area of communication and was then put down by her curt reply: *"You cannot communicate."* I knew this and sat down very sheepishly, never again to 'share' as it was called. I found the time very moving, having strong feelings of empathy with the participants going through their years of confused lives, without trying to analyse the Est structure, as some do. Things such as how much they are getting cash wise from the two weekends (multiply £350 three hundred and fifty times, which was how much it cost for two weekends and one Wednesday midweek get together). I chose instead to assess what I had achieved in that first weekend. I was told that the coming week would produce "Breakthrough" - this will be when you will 'get it'. Woody Allen referred negatively to 'est.' trainings in his films, taking a side swipe at its substance. The trainings were geared towards community leaders, who would later influence others with their new-found wisdom after breaking free from years of conditioned thinking about making partners, family, management, wrong. The reason for the programme was for 'Transformation', mainly in the area of relationships.

After five years I did the second training, under a new structure called 'The Forum', in 1985 (I believe). I found the first day a far less confronting experience than the earlier 'Training'. This time the leader was an Austrian American fellow who, from the beginning, had a problem with a Jewish participant who could not free himself by associating him with the Holocaust and Hitler. On perhaps the third day we came to the part of the training where you share any issues in regard to your life. These were described as 'Items' on this occasion. Prior to the food break, he said to come back ready to share the 'Item' with the group. I had made up my mind to say something about myself, no matter what, for this was my second time round and I had spent seven hundred pounds of hard-earned money, so I was determined not to let this opportunity go by.

As we settled down in anticipation of the coming session in the Ballroom at the Cumberland Hotel, Marble Arch, we were asked to raise a hand to share our item. My hand went up as I shook on the seat, petrified like some blob of shaking jelly, listening to my voice that came from somewhere, stumbling over the words and standing up to speak into the offered microphone. I perceived the staff sitting around the room, separated from the main body, as my accusers. Accusers whom I saw as members of the public reflecting the guilt I felt over the crimes I had committed. I spoke of my wartime experiences - having to look after the family while my mother was away, while bombs dropped, when we were in the shelter. I shook with fear as I told the story, crying my eyes out, relieved at last to be relating the despair I had endured as a child. I could not see a dry eye anywhere around me as I spoke, stumbling out my background and pain.

I was congratulated on my contribution and asked by the Trainer if anyone had ever recognised me for what I had done, looking after my siblings during those frightening times. I answered *'No'* through more tears, for this at last was my first recognition by so many people after all the years of persecution and for my actions in crime.

It was the hardest thing I had ever done in my life, but of course did what I set out to do, to share the 'Item.' I have since learnt that, in part of the Alcoholics Anonymous 'Twelve Steps' teaching, you have to expurgate your painful experiences in order to move forward. Doing this in The Training helped me considerably to lay my phantoms.

There was a point later that weekend when he spoke of life being determined - we live and die, grow from infancy, marry – and not being able to avoid cause and effect. He may have asked for questions with regard to his point of view. I said that I had an experience which in no way was determined since I had experienced, when in prison, something that was completely life changing without any pre-determined connection from a past experience. I then explained in more detail, recounting my breakdown and despair and experience of love for those that I had previously hated. He came over to me and put his arms around me in a most heartfelt embrace. He realised that something very powerful had happened to me and no-one could deny it with any logical explanation. Another important breakthrough which they also focused on, which I believe also came from the AA teaching is to take 'Responsibility' for what happens to you. Taking responsibility and forgiveness are very much bedfellows, as I realised when forgiving the police and my mother for her actions, for this allowed me freedom from blame and making wrong.

This comes from a change in consciousness, as Jesus on the Cross saying, *"Forgive them, for they know not what they do"*. A true example I heard was shared by one of the participants who had his day-old car badly damaged when someone ploughed into the back of him as he was waiting at traffic lights. The man and his wife got out of the front car to take down details, much to the bewilderment of the driver responsible for the crash, who said, *"Why aren't you upset at me for doing this to your car?"* The fellow said because I did a 'Workshop' which helps in situations like this. The concept of responsibility is a hard one to take aboard but it does work. I once had many pieces of waste cloth in a box that bothered me, realising it was part of my profits laying there. The phrase then came to me, that *all life is profit.* I never thought of that cloth the same way again. The same can be said for many other situations in life. In the case of my imprisonment, although I was not responsible for the crime, *I was responsible for how I did the sentence.* I could have walked away as I worked on the officer's houses; I could have refused to do anything; I could have perhaps acted mad, as some did at times, or committed suicide. I could even have smeared shit over the cell walls in protest. No, I knew I had much to live for, having missed out on my past. But only when all doors were closed to me did I break down. ***Then came the Mystic Experience.***

After the 'Forum' I did many other seminars with this organisation, as well as helping prepare the room for the Training, working in the office on the records section and cross-referencing Trainers' information sheets. The latter were sent to America for statistical purposes.

After a time I formed a 'Personal Growth' group in Lewisham Unitarian Meeting House, giving away all that I had learnt over the course of my own growth. I wanted a place in South London where like-minded people could meet to share their lives, rather than having to go to North London to find groups. It was a success from the start, as there was a need for it south of the river. It lasted for a number of years until I felt it had served its purpose.

My mother was now in severe pain with arthritis and housebound, but determined to run a small greengrocer's in West Street, Erith: the same shop where I had stolen the apple as a four-year-old child, giving me such a fear of persecution about going to school. She didn't go anywhere except the shop, which was her sole interest, but remained happy to buy various pieces of gold jewellery, including any stolen pieces that Joe's friends from London might send his way.

I began to get bouts of anger and depression, which caused me to sublimate my energies in helping others. What I couldn't put right in myself I tried to put right by helping where I could. I had my mother to think about, but knew she was in good enough hands with Joe at this juncture of my life. This form of altruistic projection was the way I kept sane, coupled with working hard and playing golf to forget the problems of our marriage. My obsessive interest in golf acted as a form of escape, as an ostrich-like way of avoiding reality. This was all in my early fifties before I did the second Training. I played golf until the early 1990s, when I had to give it up through incurring a slipped disc that was to slow me down considerably, including any sexual pleasure, infrequent though it was at the time.

The Youth at Risk Project

I do not judge a man for what he is
But, by what he may become.
Albert Schweitzer

Through a friend I met during the 'Forum Training',
Margaret Cowgill, I was given a contact in London to
join a new group called the 'Youth at Risk Project',
the brainchild of an American Probation Officer who
had become disenchanted with his work, seeing the
youth return so quickly to crime. The Probation
Officer had done the Forum Training and formed the
'Youth at Risk Programme' which was given free to
the youth, from corporate funding. This was one
example of the 'Forum' having an effect on society.
Funding was offered and it had proved a runaway
success after initial teething troubles in various States.
The same thing happened here, and local authorities
were approached to offer their social workers for the
five days it took to do the training. None were willing
to try out this new American concept, where the
'Youth' would be taken away from their homes for
five days to undergo a rigid structure, resembling in
part an Outward Bound course coupled with hours of
classroom attendance, from eight in the morning until
midnight. Margaret thought I would be ideal for the
team with my background, knowing where the kids
were coming from.

Tower Hamlets in East London was first to accept the programme but, unfortunately, at the eleventh hour the whole project was scuttled, due in the main to fear of non-professionals being involved with the youth. We then had to start from scratch, arranging for meetings with other Boroughs. When Lewisham was approached, it included the Lewisham Probation Service where I was a volunteer under its then head, Ron Hatt. They had their own internal problems at the time and voiced total disagreement at the presentation, stating their staff wouldn't have any part of it without pay. The few volunteers we managed to find had to be kept interested for some eighteen months, by doing workshops, until we successfully involved the Borough of Enfield in 1993.

Approximately thirty-seven of the youth from Enfield, Edmonton, and Brixton were bussed down to Devon to a large Manor House. On arrival they were clapped as they got off the coach, in recognition of their courage to undertake the week's 'Training'. What they didn't know was that volunteers were sent in ahead to clean, paint, and repair the Training Room a week beforehand to get it in pristine condition. When the youths arrived late at night in early September, most wore hoods covering their faces. I was reminded by these dark figures of bent human question marks, with their heads hanging low, avoiding our peering eyes as they rushed into the house carrying their cases and not understanding our clapping to greet them.

At one of our early talks given by one of the American trainers, he stated we wouldn't get any appreciation or recognition for our efforts as volunteers from the youth. He was right!

I was part of the security team, watching as they entered their respective dormitories, checking the name cards denoting their bunks. Immediately the cards were switched round, naming friends they wished to be with. One room was set aside for the females who numbered around thirteen - one aged sixteen was already a mother of two children.

The American team arrived two hours later, thrilled to see the house but not the problems it gave in regard to security. Some white tape was produced and used to mark out 'no go' areas for the sexes. In each of the three dormitories, responsible adults were assigned to keep order.

The training began the next day with breaks for toilet if needed. Toilets had to be overseen by two volunteers, to verify visits were for genuine purposes. The youngest of the group was fourteen; the eldest twenty-two. None of the males wanted to be seen crying, but many did when painful memories were exposed to the class.

Whilst the first session was taking place, the head of the security team and I went through the youths' lockers and clothing looking for cigarettes, weapons and dope. I found one knife which had a seven inch blade.

A lot could be written about the Youth at Risk Project, as it was then known. I consider it the most effective way to reach the youth of the world, no matter what culture they come from. It has since been filmed on TV under the title 'Tough Love'. When the youth had their 'Pass Out Day' and were recognised for their efforts, I was moved by the transformation, having watched those disturbed, hunched human question marks alight from the coach at the beginning. And then, to hear them speak with such conviction and confidence, with heads held high, was powerful indeed.

Five years later I went to their first reunion, to find that two were soon to be Trainers, another had become an Architect. I am sure many others could achieve such recognition in their lives if they had the opportunity to face their demons under such a caring structure. When the five days are over, each youth is allocated a Committed Partner, who will have the youth phone him each week, meet once a fortnight, and come to a progress meeting once a month for the whole day for a year. Getting the youth to keep these commitments is no easy task, but it is essential for them to have goals within this structure, such as education, work, and fun time like shows, dancing, and so on.

Enfield Social Services said the most important lesson they had learnt from the five days was that they had never listened to the Youth in the past, thinking they always knew best for them. But they would most certainly listen in the future.

The Alister Hardy Research Centre and PPT

I heard about the Alister Hardy centre during the course of the notices being read at the Unitarian Meeting House, Catford one Sunday. I was eager to make myself known to this group so I could share my Maidstone experience, though I had never been willing in the past to do this with anyone. The Alister Hardy Research Centre was founded as the "Religious Experience Research Unit" in 1969 by Professor Sir Alister Hardy FRS after his retirement from the Chair of Zoology at Oxford University. Its aim is the study of religious and transcendent experience and its importance to humanity. I became a member during the re-launch of the London Group in 1987 where I met John Franklin, the Secretary, and five others at the Maria Assumpta Centre off Kensington High Street. We referred to the subject of evil during the course of the meeting and I shared what I knew of evil in my life. I spoke then of my awakening experience, which I had difficulty doing when speaking to such an erudite group. I was asked to write a dissertation for the next meeting. I did this, though with some hesitation and feelings of nervousness, being fearful answering questions which exposed my past and demons to this new body of people.

I am glad I am still a member of this group, which now has some six thousand examples on record at the

University of Wales in Lampeter, Ceredigion and I am grateful to have heard such a variety of good speakers over the years. In 1990, John and I recorded our experiences to a reporter, which were later broadcast on an Irish radio programme entitled "And Then There Was Light." Copies of the recording were sold through the Centre.

In 1993 I was filmed working on my East Street market stall and at home, giving an account of my experience in Maidstone under the title "Glimpses of God". This was repeated on BBC Television on 2nd January 1994.

I had made a contact with 'The Ashram Project' some weeks before - this group is based in Oxford and was founded by Ann Wetheral, a member of the Alister Hardy Research Centre who that realised prisoners could use their cells as Ashrams {a *Hindu word for hermitage and teaching*}. Ann had realised that with help and guidance prisoners could learn meditation and Yoga in their cells. Sadly, Ann died of cancer some weeks after I enquired about membership. I later did an introduction seminar for Yoga in prisons with the Trust and adult evening classes for Iyengar Yoga as well as Meditation techniques locally in Catford. I informed the now renamed 'The Prison Phoenix Trust's' Deputy Director, Sandy Chubb, about the soon to be shown BBC Programme in which I was to appear. I believe my TV appearance helped my credibility in teaching meditation: it documented my experience and highlighted the sincerity of my desire as an ex-offender to help others. I did eventually meet Sister Elaine McInnes, the Director of the Trust, one afternoon at Kings Cross Station where we enjoyed a short time together. On parting she gave me a gift of a small stone incense holder that I have used over the years in teaching the rudiments of Yoga Asanas. Meditation, coupled with my own input of spiritual and conscious awareness, gleaned over the years, was mixed with Buddhist and Hindu texts. I am deeply grateful to Sandy Chubb for her help in getting me started in my first prison, HMP Swaleside, Kent, a category C placement where prisoners are given above average freedom in the form of exercise and recreation.

I was there for about nine months. Unfortunately the group gradually lost attendance due to changing venues, so it had to close. Fortunately all was not lost, however, as a Yoga group has now been established there for some years with a regular venue in the Chapel.

I started at Wandsworth soon after, covering for the regular tutor, Margarita Orteza, while she had two months' holiday with her husband in Spain with their aging parents. She eventually had to return to Spain when her mother was taken ill, so gave up the class to be with her. I then took her place on a regular basis, teaching in what is known as the VPU (Vulnerable

Prisoner Unit), a prison within a prison, where the inmates are segregated for their own safety. Margarita kindly sent me a card from Spain saying how glad she was to have known me and grateful that I would be taking her place and that she would sit each Thursday to be with us all in spirit while we sat in Wandsworth.

I was now back full time in 'Wanno', this time as a teacher: a reformed crook without a blemish on my character for over thirty years – after two sentences due to police fitting me up for something I hadn't done. Was it chance and coincidence or was it something else? Could not the whole thing have been part of some elaborate scheme where I had been a leading player in some cosmic game or plan?

I went each Thursday morning at seven by car to Wanno, spent two hours taking the class (for which I never wanted payment) and was home by one. I was glad to do it, knowing that I was well received and without any doubt contributed to the lives of the inmates. One of the high points of my time there was when an American couple, Bo Lozoff and his wife Sita, came to give a talk on his work in prisons and how inmates can use their time constructively, even with serious sexual offenders, through allowing the spirit to move in the right direction. We met in the gym, seated around Bo on some of the matting, with Sister Elaine McInnes. The classes were made up of those who were interested from both the Main wings and VPU. Sandy Chubb took us through some basic

231

exercises before Sister Elaine gave a short meditation period. Bo then gave a most fascinating talk on his work in American Prisons. He is the author of a number of books on ways to live the spiritual life, his most definitive being, *'We're All Doing Time'* which is given free to prisoners who apply for it in British prisons from 'The Prison Phoenix Trust'. This book is a must for those seeking the spiritual path that are willing to rise higher than the mouse-like way most of us live, which is how Bo describes this state of ordinary being or consciousness.

Over the period of ten years that I taught in Wanno, I befriended some five ex- prisoners. Three are still free: the other two succumbed to drink and drugs within eighteen months of release and returned.

My mother died suddenly on the twelfth of April, 1994 aged eighty-four through gastro-intestinal bleeding caused by taking aspirin-based tablets given to her in error by Joe. I signed the death certificate on the thirteenth of April, again the date of my supposed crime back in 1958. She had been taken into Hospital on the twelfth with my sister Barbara, John and Joe there to say goodbye as she was taken into the emergency receiving room. We thought we would see her later in the evening so didn't kiss her goodbye. I stroked her hair as she was wheeled away from us all. She died later that night.

My mother's funeral was a very difficult time, bringing back so many painful memories of the war years. Others of her remaining sisters, knowing of her actions during the war, didn't find it any easier reliving those old feelings of guilt caused by her actions. Her brother Henry spoke to me about how it was she who had bought him his first pair of long trousers, saying he'd never forgotten it. I had to hold my brother Bob up when leaving the church, for he was in a deep state of remorse and hardly able to walk.

Joe was now in a wheelchair through advanced cancer in the lung. I believe they took the wrong one out, looking back in hindsight, for when taking him to the hospital on one occasion a doctor was confused as to which one was for removal. Joe in his humorous way said, *"Don't take the wrong one out will you"*. A few weeks after his operation, complications set in: they said a little bit of infected cancer was left in, and it had now spread to the other lung. It has been known to happen. Joe died six weeks after my mother in the hospice at Bostall Heath, Abbey Wood. Both my brothers were deeply affected by our mother's death, but John the most. He cared for them both when they were ill and took it very hard when mum died; believing the arthritis in his leg was caused by the shock.

Joe was very difficult with the black nurses when he was ill, they brought out all the racist attitudes that he had held all his life. John, being such an easy going fellow, full of compassion for them both, took a lot of stick from Joe. Joe had gained a reputation around

Erith as a character, both for his drunken escapades and stealing. He had a running battle with the owner of the butchers, who frequently caught him on his drunken forays with something in his bag he hadn't paid for. The manager of the supermarket also had the same trouble with him when under the influence. This caused quite a few sniggers in the church when the Vicar gave the eulogy, speaking about Joe's ability as a general builder and foreman when he said that, *"He was very good with his hands"*. As we left the service in our limousine, the driver couldn't understand our laughing, when we should have been so solemn. Joe left enough money in cash and building societies to have a good send off at the local pub, with his old drinking partners, plus gifts to his arch foes, the managers of various shops in Erith, that had suffered through his good humoured pilfering over the years.

Fortunately he'd saved enough money to give them all a good drink to remember him by. At the local pub free beer flowed all day - for both his friends and his enemies. We also had enough money to bury him with my mother in a part of the cemetery that held well known Travelling families.

Now both Mum and Joe had died, I found more time to do other things, such as giving more time to the Meeting House at Catford. My brother John stayed on in the flat that my mother and Joe had rented from the council. When they heard his story about caring for them both, the council had found him a place in some run-down flats in Erith, near to Uncle Bert. Uncle Bert, although now in his seventies, still regularly gave money to a twenty-year-old drug addict for her fix in return for sex. He hadn't long been out from doing his last sentence of two years for handling drugs for one of the local dealers. These things of course do happen in the murky world of crime, where deals such as this are made all the time. It wasn't long before John was burgled and his television was stolen, plus his electronic chess game that he was more upset at losing. I fixed his door for him with a new deadlock, making it secure.

One Sunday morning, the visiting preacher had forgotten about the service, so I volunteered to do it, taking the opportunity to speak about my Maidstone experience. There were about ten of us there at the time, so I quickly selected four favoured hymns for George, our organist, to play. I then commenced with the service, making it last for the statutory hour, to the satisfaction of most there.

Some years prior to taking this service I had spoken about my time in Maidstone in response to a question from the Minister, Joy Croft, about whether Myra Hindley had changed enough during her time in prison to be freed and allowed to live a normal life. [Joy was the first person with whom I had shared my experience in Maidstone]. Something must have filtered through to the whole of the congregation for, sometime later, I had a telephone call from a very disgruntled member who had been burgled, asking me for their stolen property back. I dismissed this accusation from whoever it was without any rancour on my part accepting it for what it was worth from a very upset woman.

I had assumed that my address when taking this service had cast some light on my now, changed character. I had spoken about my spiritual awakening and its effect on my life, in comparison to others who, finding it difficult to change continued to commit crimes. I took other services whilst at Catford, some better than others, for I must admit I didn't take too long setting them down as some do. One I was quite pleased with was based on Heraclitus that a previous Minister had mentioned in his address one Sunday. When he finished I thought *"I could have done that"*, for I knew of the Greek philosopher. So I revamped it to my own liking, telling the listeners what I had done, so I wasn't guilty of plagiarism.

I then did two services in Hastings, with Muriel in attendance on the first one, on her ninetieth birthday. I don't think I did too badly, but it wasn't the usual standard format for I included feedback from the congregation prior to the notices being given. I sensed this was not appreciated, but was glad to have had the honour of doing both with Muriel in attendance. Sometime later, after the then District Minister had visited Australia, he was surprised to find this was a regular practice down under.
I continued attending the Meeting House in Lewisham most Sundays, taking Greta to the wholesaler in the

morning then setting up the stall before going back to Lewisham for the service until midday. Then back to help Greta on the stall. It was a serious business having the spiritual commitment. I did this for a number of years, as well as visiting the mother of one of the members whilst her husband was in Switzerland during the week.

I have been very lucky throughout my life, having good health and strength, which has allowed me to do so much.

Charlie Goodchild when younger

My first visit for 'Lewisham Social Services' was taking a Downs Syndrome man, Charlie Goodchild and his sister for a ride as a respite trip for them both. I recall picking Charlie up from his chair like a child *[he weighed all of ten stone]*, holding him close to my face and smelling stale, partly dropped food adhering to his clothes as I carried him to the car. I put him in the front seat where we sang his favourite song, *'Singing in the Rain'* for him. Charlie was then in his sixties, which I was told was old to be a Downs Syndrome person. We would ride in the country, buying fresh farm eggs and fruit when available. He died unfortunately while having an operation for enlarged prostate trouble. Charlie and his sister were close to my heart as my first clients, so to speak, in voluntary social work.

My father was now close to retiring from a company that made office copying machines, based in Victoria. He was married to Ivy, enjoying life and having a regular income as Dispatch Manager for the firm. He'd settled down at last, well respected by his staff and superiors. Unfortunately he was still very vain, rarely visiting us and showing no interest in his grandchildren at all. The times he did visit, he would take longer looking in the mirror putting his hat on than he did talking or playing with the children. He was that kind of character I'm afraid, completely involved with himself, just as he had been with us all as kids. Whenever I got the rare letter from him in Maidstone, it was in the main about what he would have to eat, whilst watching Ivy prepare it in the kitchen. Something quite spicy and tasty, such as tender chicken, he was glad to describe - far removed from the plain prison fare I had to put up with. He would invariably end a letter by telling me the colour of the suit he was having made at Barry's in Brixton;

how it would look good with his new shirt and shoes. For a laugh I would read these letters to the painting team. He had done time himself in the past, as I have previously recorded; why didn't he realise what he was doing?

Bob had long ago taken to painting while in prison, under the tuition of John Wayne Morgan, a correspondence course art teacher, who thought Bob the best of his six hundred students; in particular his ability in capturing the female form. Bob won a number of Koestler competitions, eventually becoming one of the judges for many years, after leaving a life of crime. He did twenty years out of an aggregate of thirty from the age of nine. He was put in Wormwood Scrubs Prison at fourteen, the youngest offender known at the time, for persistently absconding from various Approved Schools and National Children's Homes. Unfortunately he inherited my father's gene: unable to handle money; being forever broke; spending it compulsively like a child; causing him many problems in later life.

My sister Barbara married, having four boys as well as a girl, Susan, from an earlier relationship at seventeen. When Susan was born it was a unifying occasion for us all, for Joe really took to this innocent baby, becoming part of our dysfunctional family. We never accepted Joe as the father figure that he, I am sure, would have liked to have been to us, but after leaving his own family of three boys in the West Bromwich area of Birmingham, Joe took to her, as if being her true grandparent, doting on her and giving her the attention and love he craved for himself: nothing was too good for her.

John married very soon after, having met a girl in a pub at Woolwich, but it wasn't a happy affair. They divorced after a lot of stress on his part through his wife's behaviour. He had a boy and two girls, one of which he has contact with now, a daughter Denise. He is at the moment living happily in sheltered accommodation in SE London, seeing his two grandchildren as often as he can.

Barbara is living in Kent with family and great-grandchildren nearby. Bob is in Sussex, partially housebound through lung trouble, but still with a long-time friend who looks after him by getting his shopping and visits when she can. He rarely paints now.

Dave Doris and Family

I first met Dave during his early years as a fly –pitcher in Woolwich, working outside the Shakespeare Pub in the High Street. This meant pitching down wherever possible to sell your wares, without having the local Bobby nick you for obstructing the footway, hence the occasional running to hide when the warning was given by the lookout to get away. We met up on the odd occasion through the course of the years, sometimes working together when we found a good line to share. Dave married Doris and had three children, all girls: Lisa, Kerry and Natalie.

I teamed up with another well known trader 'Sleepy Terry' going into the making-up business in Bermondsey. Dave did some work for us, making deliveries to outworkers of Bat Man and Robin suits, made from plastic sheeting. These were quite the rage at the time, being a series on TV. All the kids wanted them and we couldn't make them fast enough. Dave's dad was a docker. He sometimes came in to see how we were getting along, admiring our ideas and initiative working for ourselves. Dave had one sister and quite a few brothers who all worked hard and prospered in their own way. Dave unfortunately found he had a rare disease that affected his feet, making him lose all feeling in the nerve endings. The prognosis was that it would eventually affect his hands. Over the years it got worse but Dave never complained. I recall a time when he was helping me unload some heavy rolls of cloth: he never flinched when taking the larger of them, which must have caused him pain even though I'd told him not to take them. Once, when he got caught by a copper for street trading, he was made to walk with the heavy suitcase back to the nick nearly a mile away, until his shoes and feet were covered in blood. They were very apologetic when they saw the state of his feet - but still nicked him.

Dave had to go into the local hospital to have part of his foot amputated to save the rest of his leg when it turned gangrenous. He eventually finished up like Douglas Bader, with both legs cut off at the knee and two prosthetic legs attached. Through his courage he was asked by the surgeons to visit other amputees in the hospital to reassure them all was not lost, showing how he managed without legs and would give them hope for the future. I remember visiting him once while he was shaving and seeing the steel legs protruding from his boxer shorts. He just carried on as though it was a natural thing to do, asking me how I was, without any self-consciousness on his part. I was shocked to see how far the operations had advanced to the degree they had.

The hardest time came for him when they told him the disease was hereditary and ran through the female line, first showing itself during puberty. What torment he went through, knowing this could happen to his adored children. Dave told me that he went through

242

the most severe depression anyone could experience, thinking it would never lift: this black cloud of dejection. Both Dave's daughters, Lisa and Natalie, had become prey to the disease.

Dave died in his mid fifties after years of agonising pain, at times too powerful for clinics to stem. I remember him saying that all he worked for was his family, fearing he would not have long enough to make them financially secure. He certainly moved mountains, as was his character, to do it. I visited him on the odd occasion and spoke about what he had seen in his garden during the week in the way of birdlife, such as how the tits were getting along in the nest box. Dave would get really excited as he described how they had gone, on a particular day when he had been lucky enough to observe the young leave. He also found that he had a talent for drawing, even with hands that had lost their feeling because the nerve endings had been attacked by this affliction. I recall, on one visit to him, seeing how he had made a device that he attached to his pencils and brushes so he could grip them better. I have two of his ink drawings that I am forever admiring for the workmanship in them: they are more than mere works of skill and beauty when you understand the courage and pain it took him to do them. His boundless energy could not be stemmed by this affliction: he was always trying some way to create or invent something. One time he enthused over an idea he had for making wheelchairs go faster without tiring the passengers too quickly, unlike conventional chairs.

Dave had 'out of body' experiences, which he could self-induce when drifting between wakefulness and sleep. He would know exactly the right time to leave his bed and go out through the window to travel about the district above the rooftops. He said it was so real he felt the curtains brush past his body as he left the house, and that he was full-bodied, with legs, when doing this. I spoke to John Franklin, whom I knew could contact Peter Fenwick consultant Neuro Psychiatrist Emeritius to the Epilepsy Unit Maudsley Hospital particularly interested in OBES and NDES, an expert in such matters, and was asked by him to arrange an object on a roof, or in some guttering, say at my house. We should then ask him to go there when he was having the experience, and to look on the roof for the object. Unfortunately, Dave wasn't able to induce this feeling under the conditions described, so reluctantly we had to abandon the experiment. He was getting more severe pain from his body, which prevented him from concentrating on anything else.

I am glad to have known Dave and his family, especially Doris who must go though hell at times bearing such pain, seeing those she loved suffer so. I was grateful to Doris for allowing me to do a reading at Dave's funeral, saying how Dave would have liked me to do it. Choked with emotion on the day, I managed to get through it, although I felt my attempt far from perfect, as it was a difficult reading.

I think his out of body experiences gave Dave something to ponder in regard to a higher power and that, in some way, there could be more after death, in perhaps religion and a belief God. Dave was the bravest fellow I had ever met and it was a real privilege to have known him, and his family.

Leon Greenman

I met Leon during the time I was selling stretch covers in London markets. He was interested in what I sold and asked if I would supply him. I delivered small quantities to him on Saturday mornings - glad to help him out - though it wasn't a very profitable arrangement for me, having to drive to the East End and back. I arranged to take him to a wholesaler near to his market to buy a better variety. Unfortunately the wholesaler wasn't interested in Leon's small purchases so I continued to supply him. Leon had another stall in Petticoat Lane where he sold handbags. I occasionally visited him there just to have a chat. After a time he told me that he had been in Auschwitz and showed me his number: 98288. I was of course shocked to know about this incarceration of unbelievable cruelty that he had experienced. Leon said that his father had been an Antiquarian Bookseller in Holland before the war.

Leon married a Dutch girl, Esther and they had a son Barney. Esther's parents were Dutch and lived in Rotterdam until they were all betrayed by the local police and eventually transported to Auschwitz, where Esther and Barney perished. I remember Leon saying to me one day, as we stood by his stall, that he hated the sound of German being spoken near him.

One day he took me to his house in the Upton Park area of the East End. He showed me a small tin containing some blonde hair from his son Barney. He had an old battered suitcase with other articles that I believe came from the death camps. I was once again privileged to be shown these personal effects he'd kept over the years. I also remember once asking him for some string to tie something. He took out a tobacco-sized tin which contained an assortment of objects, extricating some string. He said that the most important of the articles was his spoon, a thing you dared not lose. Having the tin to keep articles in was a habit he didn't forget from the camps.   Leon also told me how, when speaking to (say) a Women's Institute or their like, he would sometimes get annoyed after talking about the barbarity of the camps and then, when the time for questions came, he would be asked if he ever had cigarettes. He said he gave up talking to such groups, to concentrate on schools, telling of his experiences in the hope of preventing again the rise of fascism.

Leon was eventually recognised for his efforts and dedication in speaking of his experiences, by receiving an OBE from the Queen on the twenty-fourth of February, 1998 for *Services to Community Relations*.

As friends of Leon, my wife and I attended a small party in his honour at The Holocaust Survivors' Centre after the ceremony. Now in his nineties, he has frequently been seen in television programmes, showing sixty years' remembrance of the Holocaust.

Leon had his book published in 2001 'An Englishman in Auschwitz', giving his full story from many others from the Library of Holocaust Testimonies. I am privileged to have known him and could not have written my own story without including an account of our meeting. I have since learnt that Leon passed away in 2007, aged 97.

Further Growth

Back to School

I decided when the eldest children took their exams that it was time I did something about my own education, so I enrolled for evening classes at Catford Boys School under the guidance of a young, tall, left-wing Jewish teacher with an Irish-sounding surname which escapes my memory but was something like Fitzpatrick, which I thought humorous. I took English Language and Literature, glad to have been introduced to the work of Wilfred Owen. I then started an 'A' level literature class, but gave up half way through when I realised I had no need for qualifications. I then took a second literature course at Goldsmiths College, New Cross, just for the fun of it. I also did two other writing classes, one at Catford Adult Evening Institute, another at Eltham, for the same thing. Our tutor there wrote for a TV company and was very good for the time we had her. When the class folded we formed a small group, meeting at two of the members' houses, sharing our efforts for criticism and appreciation. These classes helped me to feel socially included and to gain more confidence within groups, speaking up when the occasion arose.

In 1979 I started Sculpture at an Adult Day Class in Lewisham. I was asked by the tutor, Gerda Rubinstein, to do a seated figure. Never having had tuition in making anything in clay before, I had to ask others how to start the first process. This was to make an armature from aluminium wire. Again, this was new to me, so I attempted to make a skeletal shape with the wire, in the form of a seated man. I found a discarded Coke tin, covered it with a clay skin and then put lines in it with a wooden spatula, giving it an appearance of bark on a tree stump. I placed the armature on the top and filled the shape with clay, forming a head and limbs. I then decided to make my figure into a boxer, thereby avoiding the difficult parts such as fingers and facial features like ears, nose and so on, all of which were disguised by creating cauliflower ears flat to the head, a broken nose, coupled with boxing gloves to hide the hands. In all, it took me approximately sixty hours to complete the whole process after which I returned to work for the Christmas rush in the market. I did some of the work at home, during the latter stages of the boxer figure, so was able to wrap the clay in sacking, putting it in a manhole until I could find time to rejoin the group.

I started again twelve years later, at a class in Deptford, led by a pupil of Gerda's known as Emma Povier. She was very good: she taught me how to make moulds from my own work. I now concentrated fully on making clay figures - one day per week for two years. Then I returned to Gerda in Greenwich and Eltham, ending my sculpture tuition when she retired from teaching sometime in the mid nineties. She had a good send-off party and get-together, where many of her students drank to her future, thanking her for the contribution she had made to our lives - mine in particular. I was never to forget her oft-repeated injunction '...*Keep Looking, Keep Looking*'. I did this at all times, gaining a deeper appreciation for the female form, which in Freudian terms is nothing more than sexual sublimation.

Muriel was taken ill sometime in 1996 and had to go into a Care Home for the partially sighted in Hastings. It was a very sad day, taking her from the home she had shared with Denbigh, her husband, for many years. He had died some years previously, after serving as Minster to the Hastings Unitarian Church for fifty years. I was with her at his funeral, holding her close for support during the time we had to walk together. I was glad to have been with her on this sad occasion.

I brought my van down on the day to help move in and carried her bed, plus other articles of importance she required, including two sculptures I had given her. I was assisted in helping her settle in by Margaret Kirk, a long-standing friend of Muriel's, and Roy Chattergee, a member of the Church and good friend of Muriel's who had been looking after her for some months prior to her decision.

It was sad to see a woman of her intellect become so dependent on the staff in the home and left to vegetate on a chair all day. We all three feared this would be the life she would be subject to once in the home.

Muriel was there for four years until she died in December 1999. I visited her each week, then each fortnight, and once a month towards the end. I saw the seasons change when I visited by train, watching primroses come and go along the banks of the railway cuttings, describing my journeys when I met her each week. I would stroke her forehead and hair, which she loved me to do for her. Most times we would be in a separate room, grateful for the privacy of being together.

I would read to her from the Unitarian Enquirer, keeping her in touch with old friends or events I thought would be of interest her. She had been a contributor for fifty years, writing articles and poems of deep spiritual insight, admired by many outside the Unitarian Church, including John Stewart Collis with whom she had corresponded for many years.

During the course of her last year in care I took some photos and measurements of her head whilst she was sitting up in bed. This enabled me to sculpt at home in my leisure. I did this despite Muriel's embarrassment about her age and looks - of course I wanted to capture the truth of how I remembered her, with love.

I had a little trouble with the structure, so I decided to make two relief profiles, each to be sited in one of the two churches most important to her - Hastings and Maidstone.

Unfortunately I could not attend her funeral, for my daughter and family had arranged for a Naming Ceremony to take place in Ireland where my reading for my granddaughter was from one of Muriel's poems.

I did speak at the Memorial Service for Muriel on the 8th of April, 2000 and recounted how we first met in the prison at Maidstone and her response when I was re–arrested for the bus stop incident shortly after leaving. It all went very well when I recounted Muriel's remark, *"Yes! Ron is a little high spirited."* This caused laughter and added a little welcome, light relief to the occasion.

What I didn't say was that I had mistakenly confused her with someone who was there to help free me from the place on account of my wrongful imprisonment. But both Muriel and Len helped instead to free me from my background and this of course was far more important.

After missing the funeral I was glad to have spoken at the Memorial Service for Muriel. It was held in a Quaker Hall and I was glad to have been able to sit at the front, so I could cry without being seen - when singing hymns and hearing others speak of the effect she had on their lives.

Criminal Case Review Commission

True justice is the righting of injustice.

In 1998 I applied to the Commission to have my case reviewed. I was told it would be put on file after I completed a formal questionnaire, which I wrote in my usual longhand scrawl. I suppose in doing this I gave the impression of being somewhat half-hearted toward it in a way. Also, I declined the assistance of a solicitor to present it, on account of the way they had acted in the past. I still retain a very low opinion of them.

I felt I had a moral duty to expose the police for what they were, after they influenced my defence by stating in the letter I read, before the trial, that I was guilty. I would have liked some form of redress and compensation because I was finding money difficult to come by at that time. Coupled with added expenses I had had a demand from the Inland Revenue which didn't help matters. I was angry at the cavalier manner in which I was treated by the Revenue, implying I was a cheat, when, in all honesty, I had made basic mistakes. I was accused of not declaring the right figures - this was because of my innumeracy.

When I eventually received the reply from the Commission in August 2000, I was not too surprised by the report they gave, stating that ... *no record of my case could be found at the Home Office, or from Crown Prosecution Service, Dorset Police, or the Court Service. None of the mentioned bodies had records or files relating to my case, as they had been routinely destroyed.*

The most glaring mistake was their assumption that the Dorset Police would have had any records or files relating to my case. That was obvious, because they had nothing to do with my arrest or conviction both of which had been processed by the Surrey Police. I was given 28 days to contact them again if I had any new evidence. I felt once again the ineptness of the Commission after two years expecting help with the case and not even getting a letter or phone call relating to the questionnaire.

Once again Muriel had helped me by sending Roy Chattergee with a cheque for the tax debt that I had been faced with two years previously and which was now thankfully settled. Muriel had enclosed a note explaining the reason she wanted me to have the money, because the tax man would have had it later in Death Duty. I phoned her immediately Roy gave it to me, thanking her for her generosity and explaining that it was now resolved. She was, however, quite adamant I should have it. This was on March 9, 1994. I still have the letter.

When Muriel's estate was finalised, we were all shocked, as it amounted to far more than we expected, with bequests to some 40 friends. I was once again grateful to have received her generous gift, which helped when I was in need of it. We all thought that she and Denbigh should have spent more on themselves during the course of their lives, which they both lived so frugally. Her letter ends by saying, '... *please accept the enclosed and give me enormous pleasure now. My love, as always, and thank you for everything. Muriel'* She obviously found this letter difficult to write because she didn't write in her usual italic script, which was always a pleasure to read. I was deeply saddened to note her loss of this ability. She unfortunately became unable to use the phone, unlock her front door, or prepare food. It was then that we sadly decided there was no other alternative but for her to go into care.

About two years after this, Len was taken ill with a stroke. Monica, his wife, phoned to tell me he was partially conscious and soon to have his hundredth birthday. I had been a fairly frequent visitor since my time in Maidstone, taking Len out on occasion. He would proudly show me around outlaying areas of Marden, his place of birth, where Monica, incidentally, had difficulty finding a grave for him in the local cemetery - probably because of his age and the loss of his birth records.

Len had married Monica, his second wife, soon after my release from Maidstone. I had the privilege of being his best man but when the time came for me to say something I just froze, unable to open my mouth, ignorant of what I had to do, never having been in a church for such an occasion.

Len disliked the nurses washing his face while I was there with him. He created such a rumpus. Monica said he was always angry when they did it, being an old sailor and the last survivor of the battle of Jutland. I contacted Trinity House to explain Len's condition in the hope that, perhaps, he would regain consciousness on his birthday, and for someone to be sent to see him. Some years earlier he had received a medal from the Queen for his work as a prison visitor for twenty-five years. A Commodore came to read a commendation, or something akin to it, for being involved in the battle and to give him Admiralty recognition as the last remaining sailor of that battle. Unfortunately, whilst I was there, Len didn't appear to be conscious, so he was not aware of the proceedings taking place. I had lost a very dear friend, who supported me, along with many others, during the course of his long and full life. He was forever a Socialist and defender of the underdog, whose life was influenced by the brutal treatment he had experienced when serving on the old training ship the 'Arethusa.'

At the time of writing, Monica is ninety-five, still living in Maidstone but sadly now in poor health. I had in the past taken Monica to Len's grave to place artificial flowers, as she was unable to use taxis because of leg problems and the need for someone to support her on the short walk. I took along a folding chair for her, where she could sit quietly for a while in remembrance while I cleaned the stone.

Since I moved from our house in London to a smaller property in the country I have given up driving distances and have not been able to visit either Len's or my mother's graves. I contacted Monica, explaining why I cannot travel anymore, having lost my nerve for driving my old car long distances. Writing my life story has taken priority over my time, being in my seventy-fifth year, aware of my advancing years and the need to get it written.

I went to Australia in November 1996 to give away my daughter in marriage. The wedding ceremony took place on Bronte Beach, Coogee, just outside Sydney, on a day with a slightly nippy breeze. A string trio accompanied the ceremony - all very romantic - coupled with breaking surf in the background and Oonagh looking radiant in white.
I just about managed to put together a more or less off the cuff speech for the occasion, joking later at the reception about how ugly she was as a child and how I would hide her from the neighbours to hide our embarrassment.

It was a rather large reception, with Greta's brother and sister-in-law over from England and so many of Oonagh's friends from Australia, as well as Greta's relations who emigrated to Oz in the fifties. Both of our other daughters, Leah and Donna, were over there also, working as waitresses in two restaurants.

I took a trip to the Northern Territories for five days, roughing it in Darwin at a youth hostel. Then, with an Ozzie guide, two Dutch girls, a German couple, and two young Japanese fellows who never spoke to each other throughout the entire journey, I took time off to see the natural wonders and beauty of the outback for three days, admiring the rugged terrain.

Looking for Unitarians in the telephone directory I was surprised to see the number of churches under the Unity denomination. I did eventually find a Unitarian Church very near Sydney and paid a few visits for the time I was there. They were undergoing some internal leadership problems at the time so felt uncomfortable during my visits, but I was grateful to have seen their Church and sent them good wishes from our Lewisham congregation.

I noticed a marked difference from Greta toward me when we returned, sensing that something had taken place with her during the six weeks I had been away. One of the fellows who worked in the wholesalers said that she was often seen with another trader with whom she had become friendly. Greta has that gregarious nature, being a Gemini, and I began to feel her becoming distant towards me, causing feelings of paranoia. I began to suspect her of deceiving me when going to Bingo, so one night I waited for her to leave the place but never saw her. She came back home later than usual and, dissatisfied with her answers to my questions, I lost my temper. I pushed her around a bit - not serious about hurting her but acting like some gorilla, breaking her plants and letting off steam by shouting. Donna came to remonstrate with me, pleading to stop my wild outburst - which I did.

I hadn't been sleeping with Greta for sometime, owing to my prostate problems and my need to get out of bed frequently. Now we became even more distant.

She rarely held me close for she had the habit of putting her fingers in her mouth to get to sleep, so slept curled in the foetal position. I always found comfort in being close to her, holding her tight to me. I realised that the finger sucking was caused by her being left as a baby on her own, as her mother was a devotee of the methods of the renowned Dr Spock whose teachings at the time forbade contact with infants when crying. In consequence, Greta unfortunately never had the close bonding that I had as a child. The Church also had caused her deep fears with its stance on Limbo, Hell and Damnation causing her nightmares at the age of nine. Sex she had been told was only for procreation and she later explained that my vasectomy was the reason for her coldness toward me.

I volunteered to go for some counselling, feeling guilty about my ranting. I had six sessions with a woman counsellor, who helped to some degree, but l became ever more distant. Greta had taken a course in assertiveness at one time, which could have contributed to her growing further away from me. She became very bolshie, doing her own thing, saving her money from work to use for holidays with friends and Bingo partner.

We slept in different rooms, growing more distant from each other. I associated her actions with the observations of Jung, who suggested that some women, when reaching middle age, adopt aggressive states and become difficult to live with. That seemed about right to me at the time. We rarely spoke as we drove to work in the market, or had any contact at all. I put the following together, expressing my thoughts at the time:

The children are gone.
We sleep in different rooms,
She sits in a chair opposite
Reading a who done it
I watch pensively;
Wondering, who is murdering who?

I found a group quite by accident after picking up a flyer from St James, Piccadilly, which was about a dance. I went to the introduction and was hooked from the start. It filled a space in my life that I needed - that of intimacy. The founder, Rolando Toro, an Argentinean Psychologist, found the format he'd devised was most successful in treating emotional needs. He described his classes as *poetic encounters*, which I think is very appropriate for you bring to these meetings your own soul. The encounter with another, spirit to spirit, reminded me of Emlyn Williams's book 'How Green is my Valley' when the young man says, *"When I go down the mine and rub my hands along the seam of the coal I am reminded where the grass is green."* When in the dance I would feel the soft skin of one of the younger females, and look into the eyes of such a beauty, I was transported to the highest of pleasures. There is nothing more moving than experiencing this sensual experience with a perfect stranger, and then to kiss this adorable woman in unbounded joy, where soul touches soul. Then to share this encounter again with another, each encapsulated in the moment, is pure joy itself. Then later to experience this unity with the whole group is never forgotten. When I first joined, I thought every church in the country should have this at some time during the week, instead of the staid traditional services we are supposed to enjoy.

I have also thought what a difference it would make to prisons, for so many prisoners have serious relationship problems with the opposite sex. Over the time I was there I was inspired to do two sculpted figures of the tutor, in appreciation and gratitude for what the encounters had given me.

A little Work, for a Charity

That which you truly own, you give away Zen

I was impressed by a short talk given by a young man Jonathan, at an Alister Hardy Society London Group meeting. I discovered that a seminar would be taking place in Brighton and I would be welcome to attend. I eventually managed to get there, volunteering to work in nine acres of gardens, removing brambles on Wednesdays from nine to five with an hour break. I was in full agreement with the ideals of the founder and his consciousness-changing ideas.

After the summer I helped to make nest boxes with another member of the group, to be sold the following spring. All the wood and nails to do this was to be donated to the charity by asking various businesses to contribute what they could. We used a room in the house as a workshop on Wednesday evenings. I shaved my beard off after thirty years, to get sponsors for the charity. I also contributed from other work I did as a handyman: together this amounted to about a thousand pounds.

As it was nearing Christmas, I joined the team one Saturday in Croydon Shopping Centre, shaking a tin on behalf of the charity to save threatened animals, while Greta did what she could on the stall in East Street. I got a shopkeeper to agree to sell cards for the

Group. Two of the members slept overnight in our house, to be early for a good pitch in a local Car Boot Sale. This wasn't much of an input compared to the efforts made by the leader who, single-handed, had collected a very large sum for 'Famine Relief'. As founder of this new consciousness-changing group, he set high standards - a combination of heart and mind coupled with a deep commitment to the new thinking. This he described as being very close to Buddhist teachings.

I only hope that the group has prospered, with a growing membership fulfilling the ideals of the founder.

However, on the morning I arrived in the market to collect the money for the charity with my now shaven face, I had a short altercation with the young son of a stallholder whilst manoeuvring the van close to his stall. I was annoyed at the young fellow for his attitude toward me and told him not to take liberties with me, old as I was. After unloading the van I overheard a remark made about me by a fellow whom I had little time for. I just snapped, still angry over the previous upset, and went for him, hitting him full in the face with my head and throwing punches as he tried to avoid me. I was pulled away by other traders, though I was angry about a trick he'd previously played on me and other stall holders. This injustice he had done to me and others had been niggling me for about a year and his remark was all I needed for me to act. It didn't help that I had not had sexual experience for a number of years and was still living a separate life from Greta, experiencing feelings of paranoia over my suspicions about her finding someone else. Although I had the problem of an enlarged prostate gland, it didn't prevent a high testosterone level which could have had a lot to do with my anger. A market can be an aggressive place and I am glad to be shot of it.

Greta cried over my action and the embarrassment it caused her, having a sixty-five year-old husband act as I did, perhaps having to suffer my temper for years to come. She asked me to go and apologise to him, but I made it look as if I had, telling him I wouldn't tell anyone about the con he'd pulled on the others with the football sweep. I never said I was sorry.

The reader will no doubt wonder how I could have behaved in such a manner at an advanced stage of my life, living the lessons learnt in Maidstone by showing compassion for the underdog. Why couldn't I forgive the young cheat who conned his fellow traders and me? Acting the way I did doesn't warrant being included under the heading of *'Growth'*. In Buddhist teaching, to lose ones temper is like going back a thousand miles in the journey to enlightenment. All I can say is that once again it was due to the injustice of it. Were those he'd robbed worthy of something?

I waited for an hour or two and then went of to collect the money from the sponsors, with the help of an article I had arranged with a local newspaper, stating it was for an animal charity.

Once again I had given an account of my past as a safe blower, much to the interest of my fellow market traders. It certainly helped in getting a good response to the charitable appeal, as well as partly freeing me once again from my past.

It was 1997 and Oonagh, our eldest daughter, had settled in Australia while our other two daughters, Donna and Leah, had partners. James was still living with us off and on. I was busying myself with building work, painting and decorating as well as working on the house and garden in preparation for selling it. By now I had given the prison class over to another teacher, in readiness for the move from London. I cut down my time working in the market to weekends only. I concentrated on the house decorating, renewing all the windowsills. I discarded three vanloads of rubbish during the repairs before I was satisfied it was good enough to sell. I enjoyed working with my hands, having to solve the small problems I encountered, doing something different. I painted the front of the Unitarian Meeting House and did some other repairs, leaving it in good condition. I also worked on a neighbour's chimney stack, re-seating and pointing it during the course of a week. It was hard going but enjoyable. At 71 I knew it to be my last work as a paid handyman. I was still strong enough to climb the three ladders to the roof, carrying full buckets of cement to point the stack. I paced myself, working five hours a day, grateful for having the strength to do it.

Retirement 2004

We stored our furniture and moved to a rented cottage in the country, where the bells of a nearby church rang out a welcome each Wednesday evening and Sunday morning. I was glad at last to have left London and work behind. In the ensuing months I looked for suitable properties that would not eat too deeply into our adequate nest egg.

We looked at some twenty properties in our price range, before finding the right one. It had all we wanted in the house except for some rooms that needed attention, which I was capable of putting right with little effort. We moved in on the twenty-seventh of November, 2004 with the help of the family, all mucking in to help. Kevin brought the furniture from storage in a van from a local hire company and all took part in the unloading. Both Leah and Donna now lived nearby with their partners and children, so all was now ready for our life of comparative leisure.

I had also given a dozen or so of my sculptures to the Prison Phoenix Trust before leaving, which were to be auctioned at a venue in Oxford. Earlier in the year, on the twenty-fourth of March, I went to Oxford carrying a spare piece of sculpture in an overnight bag, to be added to those already on display for the auction to be held at Corpus Christi College that evening. There were other donations from prisons and gifts from a variety of London shops. I was surprised at the amount of work that had been done behind the scenes by Sandy and others from the Trust.

Giving a thumbnail sketch of my background, Sandy the director introduced me as a generous fellow. I remember getting up without thanking her for her kind words, and then had a panic attack, not knowing what to say until Sandy reminded me to speak about introducing flowers to the meditation classes. I remember finishing the talk saying that I intended to write my life story during the coming year.

The Auction was then professionally conducted by Charlie Ross, the television personality from *'Flog It'* who kindly did the whole thing for nothing. He even bought one of my relief owl pieces for himself. The following day I went for a short walk through some fields with Sandy and her husband John, hearing the welcoming sound of larks singing. I was grateful to have shared time with Sandy and her family, but still felt put out by my inept attempt at making a speech. Nevertheless, I was bucked by the response I had received for my sculpted animal figures. One was of two birds perched on the handle of a garden implement, which I captioned, *'you sing it, while I'll hum it'*. The thrilled purchaser, a writer, told me of a publisher to contact once I had finished the book.

While writing this book, I have had one or two experiences relating to coincidences that I believe are meant for a purpose.

Prior to our move from Lewisham, I visited a writing and poetry group where a member spoke of visiting our intended town to read her poetry for an annual competition. When at my last Biodanza group, I spoke to a fellow who lived in the county we proposed to move to. I asked him the town he came from. It transpired he lived a stone's throw from my daughter and was responsible for designing the poetry group's new building.

When writing the section describing handcuffs being sawn from Israel Small's wrists by my step-grandfather, I closed down the computer at that juncture and set off to cycle to a nearby town. Making my way to a river towpath I found the pathways under repair so had to find an alternative route. I stopped a woman jogger to ask the way and she directed me to some crossroads where I saw the direction to take. I chose another path which led to a bridleway that looked more inviting, leading to the opposite river bank - rather overgrown but with interesting views of fields to my right.

After a while I came to a road and met a stoutish middle aged man walking toward me. I dismounted to ask if I was on the right road for the town. He gave me the directions then asked if I had seen a gate leading to the river. I told him I had, and how far away it was. He then told me that he had not been along the road before, as he was the new secretary of the local Angling Club and wanted to try a key in the gate lock to see if it fitted. After some general conversation regarding what part of London we had each lived in prior to moving into the county, it transpired he had lived in Edmonton, going to the same school as Israel's son and knowing of his gangster background. This took place within forty minutes of my leaving our new house, closing down the computer and meeting a man who knew the fellow whom I had just written about. Neither of us knew the area, but somehow we were destined to meet in an uncanny way, the odds of which would be millions to one.

Once again I can only believe this to be the work of another power beyond that of our rational mind. I am grateful to this guide or angel, which has given me such valuable insights or portents during my life journey. I am now happily enjoying my time, finding interests, visiting the local Quakers, deciding between leaving the Unitarians after so long and joining the Quakers. I am involved with some voluntary work, a Psychic Group, enjoying bird watching at last, plus seeing a lot of our grandchildren. I intend to keep writing and to take up sculpting again. Now I have completed this book, I hope it may help others struggling with disturbed psyches and perhaps wrongful incarceration. I hope it will assist those seeking help with their spiritual journeys and perhaps lay their phantoms to rest. I have observed from my own actions, and those of others, that when you move in the right direction the universe and God move with you.

Postscript

Only the intelligent benefit from suffering
Somerset Maugham?

Having joined a local group, I needed to get clearance from the police to do voluntary work. In authorising this I was told the wrong button had been pressed - I agreed it was OK for the organisation to have a full account of my record, rather than the shorter version that would have been legally adequate. Unfortunately this gave the whole of my criminal history from my school days dating from October 1945.

Nevertheless, when they took me off the duty rota, I was naturally disheartened that past offences should come back to haunt me after fifty years. Knowing how far I had left my past behind me, this did rancour to some degree. However, the process of looking back over the police files and the records was helpful for me in writing this book - through giving exact dates I had long forgotten. Thankfully, head office in their wisdom decided eventually that I should be reinstated and to carry on as usual with my duties, including ongoing training each year.

I have also discovered that most of my anger has been directed towards feelings of injustice, not only towards me but to others in a capacity of caring, by putting myself on the line by doing it. The Forestal situation was one, when I got seven days banged up for it, and the last example was my striking the fellow who cheated his fellow traders. Striking my mother and the bottle situation was done to protect my siblings in a nurturing way. There are other examples in the book.

On reflection, I feel that there has been a pattern or plan to my life, which led me towards the mystical experience in Maidstone. From the time I saved the fellow's life on Chiswick Station, aged seventeen, and heard that voice saying, "g*o away you will be rewarded.*" Again, in the identification parade, something similar occurred with a voice saying, *"look at him, and let's get it over with."*

It's a strange form of deliverance. In my confused state, I had no recall of the time my friend Jim Thorne came to borrow a wallpapering brush from me, when I was supposed to have been involved in the car accident at Brentford. I truly believe that this power, whatever it may be called - God, Karma, or divine retribution for the crime I had committed in Shepherds Bush - is real. How was it all connected? I do not feel it was a coincidence that I found the 'Perennial Philosophy' when in Wandsworth, waiting for transfer to Maidstone [this was one of Muriel's favourite books]. Reading from it, this phrase of Eckhart says so much:

You talk to me of miracles, if you could fly, you would accomplish no more than a bee.

If you could walk on water, no more than a piece of straw.
If you really want to achieve something then go within yourself.

I realised that when you truly know yourself, self disappears to become part of the whole, as in the Buddhist sense, *as a raindrop merging with the ocean connected to everything.*

Blake's words are also profound with his observation that *we see the universe in a grain of sand;* because the universe forms that grain of sand.

Swimme and Berry say the same thing in The Universe Story:
The eye that sees the Milky Way was made by the Milky Way.

This connection to all life leads me to believe there is no death, as in Schopenhauer's observation that *man is a mortal leaf on an immortal tree,* our spirit lives on. That is why I became aware of my life connection, when I say that I was born at the beginning of time, I find it inconceivable that it should ever end: being part of the whole, from the creation of the universe to the present moment.
Do we have angels or guides during the course of our lives?
From my own experience I can only accept it as more than chance.

The fact that I've had too many uncanny coincidences occur throughout my life seems to lead to this possibility. The most significant was the birth of my daughter, Oonagh, born on the same day the crimes were committed [*the crimes for which I was wrongly sentenced*] some years later. Paradoxically, I see this as a gift for what I experienced as a child during the war - the mental pain suffered during the time in Maidstone and Winchester after the solicitor reneged on his word to appeal for me. I wasn't able to accept the sentence as poetic justice for the crime I had committed, because I didn't consider myself an active criminal. I had no intention of committing other crimes, feeling doubly angered after having found some semblance of happiness with Ann, after Shirley had left me. With the benefit of hindsight, following my change of consciousness in Maidstone, I now see I deserved the sentence as a form of psychic retribution to change my behaviour. I should never have taken Ann for the abortion, mixed with the characters in Woolwich, committed the Shepherds Bush crime, or stolen motorcycles when returning to Acton and Irma. I deserved it for not trying hard enough to unravel my psyche.

So, belief in a higher power or arbiter – that moved me towards the baptism and conversion where I am today.

Having gained so much from my imprisonment, what compensation for wrongful incarceration could equal it? I have been given the most powerful experience man can have; there's nothing to compare with it. As stated earlier, I have seen beyond the normal state of consciousness to that of abounding love. What redress can compare to that of finding the power of love and God?

Epilogue

On New Years Eve 2009, I went with a friend to a
Bonanza Meeting; enjoying dancing with new and old
partners at this annual event, my first for this particular
occasion. Arriving home late and arranging a bed for a
friend who needed a place to stay, slept late. Seeing the
friend on the train in the morning; I rode my bike to a
Nature Reserve checking bird feeders as a volunteer for
a charity; a far cry from the opening chapter;
confirming my now long interest and care for birds, due
to compassion for life in later years. Descending a
bridge onto a towpath, by the river Lee, I bent over to
attach bike clips, checking behind to see all was clear,
rode off. The next thing I remember was the river
coming toward me very fast and unable to break, or
steer away, before hitting it hard face first, from
a height of about six feet and feeling the impact and the
shock of the freezing water. I must have lost
consciousness immediately I started off on the bike
travelling about a hundred yards before going into the
river. Were the actions of the previous night too much
for my age contributing to the following? . I swam to
the side grabbing one of the wooden boards above the
water level. My sheepskin, lined coat was now far too
heavy to attempt getting out. I also had a
rucksack strapped to my back, containing binoculars
and other items giving extra weight. Making
it impossible, to raise myself above the plank or my leg
to the path, for leverage to rise higher. Two cyclists

eventually came to my aid struggled to get me onto the path. After walking with them short way was asked by two other fellows if I needed a lift home, when learning I'd fallen in the river and to go with them to the taller chap's house. I was now beginning to feel in shock, after walking a fair way to his house; a blanket was soon placed around me then was driven to my home. I was glad to get in the warmth of the house after thanking the fellows for their help and then a duvet placed around me by Greta and a couple of hot drinks after which a quick shower and then a sleep. I cannot understand why I blacked out prior to falling into the river but grateful for it happening; taking it as a- wake - up call spurning me on to finish the book, getting dejected with rejection slips. It also tallied to eight on near death experiences, over the course of my life. I realise at 77 shall not have many years left; at the rate I'm going. . 1 have been influenced by the dictum of Heraclitus; saying we cannot step twice in the same river. We are all in the state of change from birth until death. We cannot say when seeing a photo of the past; this is of me, because we have only the memory of that event and have no other connection during our journey of metamorphosis. Each second of each day is a different state of being, that is why eternity is now and now and now.

Observations

'What to the ordinary man is light to the seer is darkness' Buddhist text.

'Man blindly taps with his white stick of consciousness along the corridors of time oblivious to Gods greatest gift the miracle of his own existence. '

'One act of unconditional love is worth more than a lifetime of solicitous piety .'

The above insights have come to me during contemplation and meditation during the course of my life in the knowledge that when you have obtained enlightenment one is able to enfold the problems and difficulties into the vastness of the new found consciousness.

For the last four years have been a volunteer with a national charity. After three as an attendee Quaker, have now been accepted into membership, of the Area Meeting of the Religious Society of Friends.

Acknowledgements

To my mother, for what she had to endure for us all. Our Grandmother for love care and guidance the education officer at Lewes Prison for his help in 1952. Muriel Hilton Unitarian Lay Minister and Len Powell member at Maidstone Meeting House Greta for her hanging in there when depression and paranoia returned not forgetting the prison staff who showed kindness . Richard Woolrych for volunteering to edit my rough scrawl, Marion Dante friend and author, for her encouragement when reviewing the book John Franklin Secretary of the Alister Hardy Society, Sister Elaine Mc Innes and Sandy Chubb, for their help within the Prison Phoenix Trust. To my two brother's and sister. My, five children and grandchildren. To Martin Helm for his help.

Contemporary Photo of the Author with one of
sculptures.

Lightning Source UK Ltd.
Milton Keynes UK
26 June 2010

156114UK00001B/12/P